Work without the Worker

Work without the Worker

Labour in the Age of Platform Capitalism

Phil Jones

VERSO

London • New York

First published by Verso 2021
© Phil Jones 2021

1 3 5 7 9 10 8 6 4 2

Verso
UK: 6 Meard Street, London W1F 0EG
US: 20 Jay Street, Suite 1010, Brooklyn, NY 11201
versobooks.com

Verso is the imprint of New Left Books

ISBN-13: 978-1-83976-043-3
ISBN-13: 978-1-83976-045-1 (UK EBK)
ISBN-13: 978-1-83976-046-0 (US EBK)

British Library Cataloguing in Publication Data
A catalogue record for this book is available from the British Library

Library of Congress Cataloging-in-Publication Data
A catalog record for this book is available from the Library of Congress

Typeset in Sabon by MJ & N Gavan, Truro, Cornwall
Printed and bound by CPI Group (UK) Ltd, Croydon CR0 4YY

For Isa

Contents

Contents

Introduction

The Mechanical Turk

We live in an age of technological wonder. Today, machines beat humans at chess, write pop songs and drive cars of their own volition. Automated stores allow customers to choose their shopping and walk out without using a checkout. Through tiny chips planted in the brain, machines are apparently learning to read our minds. This silicon arcadia promises to cure our poisoned planet and take us to Mars, to realise eternal life and raise humans out of dull toil to the state of the divine. It is a world of abundance and smart solutions, where convenience is only matched by luxury.

It is also a world of dubious basis, where the apparently inexorable thrust of scientific progress is merely the dream of a few tech tycoons. Dystopia, ever the bad conscience of utopia, troubles this fantasy of cybernetic harmony, which beneath its glittering surface relies on increased oppression, surveillance and atomization. Each world-historical event, whether it be financial crash or pandemic, only seems to accelerate our drift toward its centre – a 'no-touch future' – where, encouraged to avoid others, we stay in our homes, which are no longer just personal spaces but our offices, shopping centres, gyms, doctors and entertainment venues.[1] An internet of things winds its way through our sleep, meetings and heart rates, and reports each phenomenon as data, later fed back into our lives as optimised services, all provided by one platform or another. Outside of the home, the 'smart city' offers only greater surveillance, where the dispossessed live out their days as risk profiles to be policed by biometric and facial recognition technologies. A weave of algorithms wraps all bodies, spaces and institutions in a web of machinic perception, so tightly that forms of computational intelligence become quotidian to the point of invisibility. Through this imperceptible matrix of sensors, trackers and cameras, capital gains access to new materialities of code and cognition. From meteorology to biometrics, the microscopic to the cosmic, ever more life falls under the thrall of exchange. Data is transfigured into all manner of alien machines: autonomous vehicles replace taxi and truck drivers, algorithms supplant the authority of managers and diagnose cancer with accuracy greater than any doctor.

Yet, this automated dreamworld is more fantasy than reality. Behind the search engines, apps and smart devices stand workers, often those banished to the margins of our global system, who for lack of other options are forced to clean data and oversee algorithms for little more than a few cents. The feeds of Facebook and Twitter may seem to wipe away violent content with automated precision, but decisions about what constitutes pornography or hate speech are not made by algorithms. A facial recognition camera seems, of its own volition, to spot a face in a crowd, an autonomous truck to drive without human involvement. But in reality, the magic of machine learning is the grind of data labelling. Behind the cargo cult rituals of Silicon Valley is the gruelling labour of sifting hate speech, annotating images and showing algorithms how to spot a cat.

This book argues that these badly paid, psychically damaging tasks – not algorithms – are primarily what make our digital lives legible. 'Think of it as microwork, so for a penny you might pay for someone to tell you if there is a human in a photo', Jeff Bezos informed the world at the public opening of Amazon Mechanical Turk, the first and still most famous of these sites.[2] On such sites, tasks like tagging a human in an image to train artificial intelligence last for all of a minute. Even longer jobs tend to last no more than an hour. Microwork sites allow contractors to decompose larger projects into radically short pieces of work. Contractors post these 'human intelligence tasks' (HITs) to the site, which appear on the screens of thousands of workers – or 'Turkers', as they are known – who jostle to complete the tasks on a piece by piece basis. From each transaction the platform takes a 20 per cent cut. The work is carried out remotely and workers never encounter each other except as digital avatars on online forums.

A prototype for twenty-first-century work that is as empowering for capital as it is paralysing for workers, Mechanical Turk has now been emulated by competitors such as Appen, Scale and Clickworker, offering the same heady mix of clean data and cheap labour to contractors ranging from academics to capital's great modern agents – Facebook and Google. As brokers of labour arbitrage, these sites locate what Mike Davis describes as 'surplus humanity' – sections of the global populace rendered outside of the economy proper – to sporadically fulfil the needs of big tech.[3] Contracted only for the length of a given task, workers vacillate between states of employment and unemployment, and may end up working for myriad companies over the course of a day. Volatility spun as flexibility allows these sites to present themselves as the benevolent, forward-thinking guardians of a new labour compact, designed for a generation of workers who allegedly desire greater 'independence' over security and decent pay. The sole beneficiaries of this arrangement, though, are contractors – often large tech firms such as Twitter, Facebook and Google – who get to shirk the responsibilities of more standard employment. No longer classed as 'workers' but as 'freelancers', 'independent contractors' and – perhaps most egregiously – 'players', those who work on these sites forgo rights, regulations and any last vestige of bargaining power.[4]

The brutal tectonics of platform capital are reshaping the already desolate global landscape of labour into a grey hinterland of casual and petty employment. But to read much of the literature on microwork, one would think such data work is an entirely novel phenomenon. Confident assertions of 'the human cloud', 'humans-as-a-service' and 'just-in-time-labour', suggest a tiger's leap from the workaday world of yesteryear into a brave new future of 'machine-human hybridity'.[5] 'Artificial artificial intelligence' – to use the term of Jeff Bezos – suggests a high-tech pact between worker and algorithm, in a 'new economy' set for explosive growth.[6] For this reason, institutions like the World Bank have cast microwork as the latest saviour in a long line of measures promising to rescue economies of the Global South from the slow apocalypse of informal work, debtfare and rising slums.[7] If this book has one aim it is to convince the reader that microwork truly represents not the phoenix of the South but a further twist in our planetary crisis of work. Microwork is the sum of the same processes of sluggish growth, proletarianization and declining labour demand that have ballooned the informal sectors of countries such as India, Venezuela and Kenya. As we will see in the first chapter, the rising numbers on these sites are not a story of capitalist success, but a tragic chronicle of the rising numbers unable to find work in formal labour markets. They are often those housed in prisons, camps and slums, the totally jobless or underemployed – a sorry reminder of surplus humanity.

It is perhaps not surprising, then, that the number of people on these sites has boomed in the long interregnum between the crash of 2008 and the present. Though

4

no precise figures exist for how many workers undertake microwork globally, estimates now place the number at around 20 million, a large proportion of which reside in the Global South, in South America, East Asia and the Indian subcontinent.[8] Many of these workers are educated but have been cut adrift from the formal labour market.[9] Among the overeducated but underemployed workers of the Global North, numbers are rising too. In the UK, surveys suggest that as much as 5 per cent of the UK working age population use these sites at least once a week.[10] For these workers, microwork is mostly a part-time pursuit to boost hours and stagnant wages.[11] For many across the globe, however, microwork is a full-time job. A survey by the International Labour Organization (ILO) found that 36 per cent of workers regularly worked seven days per week.[12]

Judging by the numbers individual platforms claim to host, the numbers working on these sites may well be much higher than current estimations suggest. In the last decade, Clickworker alone has grown to over 2 million users, while even smaller sites like Appen now host over a million. If the workers using these platforms were classed as employees, the contracting firms would rank among the largest employers in the world today, behind only a few governments and Walmart. Somewhat staggeringly, the Chinese crowdwork platform Zhubajie boasts over 12 million users, which would make it the largest contractor of labour the world over.[13]

The growing numbers surviving on petty data work represent, for the advocates of the Washington Consensus, some of AI's unambiguous beneficiaries, a convenient counternarrative to the steady stream of media coverage predicting automation's casualties. But it turns out the lines between casualty and beneficiary are here not so clear. The call centre workers threatened by chatbots and the checkout staff by automated stores are those most likely to find themselves adrift on the storm of twenty-first-century capital, and thus forced into the grim sanctuary of online tasks.

There are still jobs, microwork's advocates will insist. But as the average wage of a 'Turker' – at less than $2/hour – shows, even if automation has not erased workers entirely, it has now pushed them to the edge of survival.[14]

This relates to the book's second major theme. Reckoned outside of humanity proper, surplus populations have long been subject to brutal state policy. But now they encounter their inhuman status in the experiments of a Silicon Valley elite. As Bezos's description of Mechanical Turk as 'artificial artificial intelligence' insinuates, workers are not treated as humans but as computational infrastructure. Application programming interfaces (APIs) that connect requesters to workers are normally used by programmers to interact with computers. Instead, on microwork sites, requesters interact with humans posing as computers. Workers disappear in the long shadow of the machine, so that requesters, particularly larger platform clients, can uphold their marketing strategies untroubled. The ploy of Facebook, Google, Amazon and the countless start-ups hoping to secure venture capital is that their business model is radically lean, hardly dependent on the risky realm of labour, and runs almost entirely on the work of complex algorithms. They promise to conclude a process predicted in the nineteenth century by Karl Marx, whereby labour is replaced as the central figure of capital's productive force by science and technology.[15] Though platforms are speeding this process along, one only need look to the dark Satanic mills of Foxconn or the Cerro Rico tin mine – 'the mountain that eats men' – to see that for now such promises remain unmet. Platforms outsource their labour to keep it off the books and hidden from users, investors and customers, to appear more technologically sophisticated than they are, and this is no more the case than it is with the data work that powers artificial intelligence.

Though data is the lifeblood of platforms, its production is not something we tend to think of. We can see an iPhone's hardware and can glean from its materiality the labour necessary for its manufacture. But we can neither see nor touch the data that moves through its software. We are never forced to encounter the fact that data must also be produced; that such an ethereal, elusive substance is the result – like hardware – of human labour. Misapprehension becomes transfiguration, as the work of hands and minds appears solely as the result of smart machines. This data fetish – figuring automated drones in place of data labellers, media feeds in place of moderators – conceals the hidden abode of automation: a growing army of workers cut loose from proper employment and spasmodically tasked with training machine learning.

To enter this abode, as Marx did the factory of the nineteenth century, this book must also explore the dark recesses of platform capitalism, a model of economy that has rapidly grown to dominance over the twenty-first century.[16] By 2019, Amazon, Facebook, Microsoft, Alphabet (Google) and Apple filled the ranks of the top five most valuable firms in the world, with the Chinese platforms Alibaba, JD and Baidu not far behind. Essential to the rise of these firms is the immense computational power they have come to wield. As digital infrastructures that provide users a space to meet, socialize, trade and consume, platforms have gained privileged access to a wealth of personal data, taken from our online browsing, GPS locations and the conversations we have on social media or those we have in front of Siri.[17] The more data these platforms amass, the more they can feed into artificial intelligence and the greater the levels of automation they can conjure.

Yet, if the 'last mile' of automation is truly here it will likely be a long one.[18] Even if Silicon Valley by some impossible leap realised its dream and automated the Congolese mines from which it draws copper, the Foxconn factories where components become computers, and the Uber taxis from which vehicles learn to drive, nearly all of the associated technologies rely on data processing – labelling, classifying and categorising – tasks for which technological solutions remain in short supply. Not only do algorithms require clean data in the first instance but once up and running they rely on constant supervision and refinement. As Lilly Irani notes, 'Human labour is necessary to configure, calibrate, and adjust automation technologies to adapt to a changing world, whether those changes are a differently shaped product or a bird that flies into the factory.'[19]

The silicon dream of fully automated luxury capitalism may be precisely that – a dream – but its aspiration haunts a twenty-first century born of crisis and chronic recession, built on collapsing democratic institutions and intermittently wracked by climate disasters and episodic bouts of austerity.[20] For now, this imagined utopia and lived dystopia move in a strange dance toward catastrophe. As chatbots advance, California burns. As a computer beats a human at chess, millions suffer the strange symptoms of zoonotic disease. Unable to grasp its historical agency and force a better world, humanity faces a future where smart taxis silently drift under a night of perpetual storm. As freak weather events and pandemics turn ever more of humanity into refugees, prisoners and economic exiles, this burden of life – unable to find purchase in the economy proper – presents itself to Silicon Valley as software code, to be used and rejected as it sees fit.

But on a number of fronts those deemed surplus are fighting back and may provide the catalyst for a better world. Alone, microworkers have struggled to organise and trouble capital in any real way. But a rising number of events suggest a joining of forces of platform workers with other sections of the dispossessed. It is to this hope that the book cautiously turns in its final pages.

1

The Surplus of Silicon Valley

A woman living in Kenya's Dadaab, among the world's largest refugee camps, wanders across the vast, dusty site to a central hut lined with computers. Like many others who have been brutally displaced and then warehoused at the margins of our global system, her days are spent toiling away for a new capitalist vanguard thousands of miles away in Silicon Valley.[1] A day's work might include labelling videos, transcribing audio or showing algorithms how to identify various photos of cats. Amid a drought of real employment, clickwork represents one of few 'formal' options for Dadaab's residents, though the work is volatile, arduous and, when waged, paid by the piece. Cramped and airless workspaces, festooned with a jumble of cables and loose wires, are the built antithesis to the near celestial campuses where the new masters of the universe reside. In the hour it takes Amazon CEO Jeff Bezos to make $13 million, a refugee earns mere cents teaching his algorithms to spot a car – each task a stretching of the gulf between the vast and growing ghettos of disposable life and a capitalist vanguard of intelligent bots and billionaire tycoons.[2] The barbaric and sublime bound in a single click.

The same economy of clicks determines the fates of refugees across the Middle East. Forced to adapt their sleeping patterns to meet the needs of firms on the other side of the planet and in different time zones, the largely Syrian population of Lebanon's Shatila camp forgo their dreams to serve those of distant capitalists.[3] Their nights are spent labelling footage of urban areas – 'house', 'shop', 'car' – labels that, in a grim twist of fate, map the streets where the labellers once lived, perhaps for automated drone systems that will later drop their payloads on those very same streets.[4] So opaque are the sites on which they labour that it is impossible to establish with any certainty the precise purpose or beneficiaries of their work. Just next door, jobless Palestinians are made the targets of M2Work, a collaborative project between Nokia and the World Bank, which aims to give 'the most underprivileged people in the world' access to new forms of microemployment.[5] Dedicated to 'job creation' in the Global South, the World Bank undoubtedly sees Palestine's 30 per cent unemployment rate as an unmissable opportunity – an untapped source of cheap labour, readily brought into the sphere of global capital by the great telecom networks on which our brave 'new economy' rests.

M2Work is only one of many 'impact sourcing' ventures that uses microwork to reach once inaccessible segments of the global workforce. The NGO Lifelong, run by the company Deepen AI, trains Syrian refugees to annotate data for the likes of Google and Amazon.[6] Similarly, the not-for-profit platform Samasource trains refugees in Uganda, Kenya and India to complete short data tasks, and actively recruits refugees to work on Amazon's Mechanical Turk.[7] The platform's motto, 'give work, not aid', perfectly encapsulates the ethos of such projects. Samasource coined the term 'microwork' to reflect the microloan projects to which it owes its ethos. Like microfinance, banking schemes that offer loans to the jobless and poor, an aggressive faith in markets as panacea justifies projects that serve only to trap nations in cycles of debt, war and poverty. Microwork comes with no rights, security or routine and pays a pittance – just enough to keep a person alive yet socially paralyzed. Stuck in camps, slums or under colonial occupation, workers are compelled to work simply to subsist under conditions of bare life.[8] This unequivocally racialized aspect to the programmes follows the logic of the prison-industrial complex, whereby surplus – primarily black – populations are incarcerated and legally compelled as part of their sentence to labour for little to no payment.[9] Similarly exploiting those confined to the economic shadows, microwork programmes represent the creep of something like a refugee-industrial complex.

It comes as little surprise that Samasource's former CEO Leilah Janah opts for the more euphemistic 'virtual assembly line' in an effort to dress up immiseration as industrious dignity.[10] Though safer than the worst informal work – and in some cases more lucrative – microwork is often still the preserve of those with nowhere else to go. The truth is that microwork programmes often target populations devastated by war, civil unrest and economic collapse, not despite their desperate circumstances – as many advocates like Janah insist – but because of them. Such organisations know that workers in Nairobi's Kibera slum or the shanty towns of Kolkatta are hardly in the position to protest low pay or meagre rights.[11]

This is the hidden abode of automation: a globally dispersed complex of refugees, slum dwellers and casualties of occupations, compelled through immiseration, or else law, to power the machine learning of companies like Google, Facebook and Amazon. Take autonomous vehicles, a growing industry for many of the biggest platforms, estimated to be worth $54 billion in 2019 and well over $550 billion by 2026.[12] So much of the labour that companies like Tesla require centres around the need for clean, annotated data to help its driverless vehicles navigate traffic. Images taken from onboard cameras contain large amounts of raw visual data, which, to become useful, must first be categorised and labelled. The labelled data then shows the car how to differentiate the urban environment and recognise everything from pedestrians and animals to road signs, traffic lights and other vehicles. Data training rarely takes place in-house. Instead, companies like Tesla outsource the work to the Global South. In 2018, more than 75 per cent of this data was labelled by Venezuelans facing the most desperate circumstances.[13] In the aftermath of the country's economic collapse, when inflation was pushing 1 million per cent, a significant number of the newly unemployed – including many former middle-class professionals – turned to microwork platforms like Hive, Scale and Mighty AI (acquired by Uber in 2019) to annotate images of urban environments, often for less than a dollar an hour. Though the anonymity granted requesters on these sites makes identifying the large companies they host close to impossible, one can speculate with some certainty that – in typical disaster capitalist style – Google, Uber and Tesla did very well out of Venezuela's crisis. Estimates suggest that most data for autonomous vehicles continues to come from the country.[14]

From victims of economic collapse to refugees and slum dwellers, platform capitalism preys on the nominally superfluous – its profits the result of a multitude of minute tasks carried out by those chronically excluded from anything that even resembles proper employment. Held by the likes of Google and Facebook at the fringes of the labour market as a permanent shadowy reserve, they are neither quite employed nor unemployed. Hired for all of a minute to show an algorithm how to identify a pedestrian, then flung back onto the reserve pile to search for another task, workers constantly oscillate between the two states.

Similarities can be found with the reserve armies of the early-twentieth-century factory system. One worker of the period describes the 'dozens of men waiting for a door to open' at 'the factory and workshop gate' turning into 'a scramble, worse than any rugby match'.[15] Yet, unlike those hoping to secure a day's labour, the scramble for online tasks achieves, at best, a few minutes' work. While platforms like Samasource are at pains to present microwork as 'the digital equivalent of basic manufacturing', the microworker – unlike the factory hand or cotton spinner – has no distinct role. Instead, a day's work may feature a disorienting array of disparate tasks, the scramble more like that of the informal sector – with survival achieved by inhabiting endless economic niches.[16] What we find is the digital equivalent of the petty proletariat, as described by Frank Snowden in his vivid depiction of nineteenth-century Naples, which could just as easily be the tragic spectacle of modern Mumbai or Nairobi:

> These men and women were not workers, but 'ragged trousered capitalists' who filled a bewildering variety of roles that baffled all efforts at quantification. A local authority termed them 'micro-industrialists'. The elite of the streets were newspaper vendors who practised only one trade year-round and enjoyed a stable remuneration. The other huxters were 'gypsy merchants', authentic nomads of the marketplace who moved from activity to activity as opportunity dictated. They were sellers of vegetables, chestnuts and shoe laces; purveyors of pizzas, mussels, recycled clothes; vendors of mineral water, corn cobs and candy. Some of the men completed their activity by acting as messenger boys, distributors of commercial leaflets or private dustmen who emptied cesspits or removed domestic waste for a few *centesimi* a week. Others acted as professional mourners paid to follow the hearses bearing the bodies of substantial citizens to the cemetery at Poggioreale.[17]

Workers on Clickworker or Mechanical Turk can expect to perform a similarly 'bewildering range' of services over the course of a single day, ranging from audio transcription, data processing and survey taking, to more obscure errands such as finding information in local fast-food eateries and posting it online. At the stranger end, workers on Mechanical Turk have been paid cents to post pictures of their feet.[18] Defined by a lack of contracts, rights, regulations, role or routine, the microworker is not so distant from the migrant who starts the day picking recycled plastic and ends selling tissues on trains. With each reliant on finding new exchanges every few minutes, survival represents an ever uncertain goal. Putting aside the boosterish bluster of institutions like the World Bank, one can see that microwork hardly represents a new solution to the South's 'job problem', but rather a formal adjunct to an already bloated informal sector.[19]

The ominous sense that platforms are powered by the nominally superfluous is hardly dispelled when we look to the Global North. Just as in the South, microwork is often the preserve of the excluded and oppressed. In a striking example, Finnish penal labour now involves training data for struggling start-ups. The recruitment company Vainu outsources tasks to prisoners that would otherwise go to Mechanical Turk, aiming to usher in, by its own lights, 'a kind of prison reform'.[20] For each task completed the government body overseeing Finnish prisons receives a payment – though there is no public record of what percentage goes to the inmates doing the tasks. Gratuitous PR efforts to present the scheme as an opportunity 'to learn a vocation' glimmer with bad faith, particularly when one considers how ephemeral, narrow and arduous the work is.[21] Just as the physically stressful labour of ploughing fields does not take the interests of prisoners as its raison d'être, the psychically damaging work of repeatedly showing an algorithm the various senses of the word 'apple' is not about the future prospects of those doing it.

Whether as the labour of the camp or prison or as workfare disguised as welfare, microwork offers a convenient way of putting a surplus of cheap labour to work, for reasons not only of profit but also discipline. In the years after the 2008 financial crisis, state governments across the US contracted Samasource to school jobseekers in online labour, primarily in Rust Belt regions where the crisis saw the nadir of ongoing state rollbacks and deindustrialization.[22] The point of the programme was to prepare the long-term unemployed for a brave new economy, where instead of full-time factory employment and demanding managers the worker should expect contingent tasks and tyrannical algorithms. That these 'training' programmes often coincide with participants accessing platforms makes it difficult to tell precisely where education ends and workfare begins.

Though perhaps an extreme example of how microwork operates in the US and Europe, the Samasource programme is revealing inasmuch as it indicates who in the Global North uses these platforms: 'laid-off teachers, mobility impaired professionals, military retirees, agoraphobic writers… [and] stay-at-home parents'.[23] Like the Syrian refugee or the slum dweller of Kolkata, many of these workers have been drawn into capital's orbit but cast outside of formal labour markets; they comprise, in the term of Karl Marx, a 'relative surplus population', a redundant mass ranging from the 'partially employed' – left without enough hours to subsist on – to the absolutely 'stagnant' – left without a wage indefinitely.[24] These dejected participants are a necessary feature of a capricious system that employs and discards as demand expands and contracts. As workers are absorbed into the labour force they become dependent on the wage relation. When labour demand drops and job opportunities shrink, the worker must still find something else to subsist on – welfare, informal work, or else beg for food and shelter. Microwork is only the latest of these dismal options.

The Jobs Apocalypse?

How, then, did we arrive at this juncture? How did we end up with a growing segment of the globe engaged in work so precarious, contingent and badly paid that it hardly differs from unemployment, a state of affairs where informal and formal labour are, by many standard measures, indistinguishable?

The story frequently told is one of robots stealing our jobs, of advances in computation and robotics creating a slack labour market, where an abundance of workers desperately compete over scarce work, meaning employers can lower wages and destroy rights, as increasing numbers of workers are banished from the system entirely.[25] This recycled fable of jobs disappearing on an apocalyptic scale not only exaggerates the capacities of current automation technologies but also forgets a salient truth: technology has always thrown jobs onto the scrap heap of history. The present moment indicates an altogether more terminal problem: the system is no longer creating enough new jobs for the growing numbers brought into the sphere of capital.[26] There is a disjuncture growing between the ever slowing rate of job creation and the ever more rapidly expanding pool of workers dependent on a wage. As stagnant growth infects the global system, workers are pushed into ever more precarious and petty service work, while capital turns to the commodification of data and speculative investments in AI futures, a prospect only promising to further expedite human superfluity.

This is a story, then, of how the lines between employment and unemployment broke down. It is one that starts with the profitability crisis of the 1970s and ends with a world run by monopolistic platforms, where profits rely as much on data expropriation as labour exploitation, where humans continue to rely on a wage increasingly absent. It is – as with all stories told about capital – a contradictory one, of new life being breathed into the system by data and AI, but also of a world economy become deathly, so impressed by its own technological symptoms that it fails to notice the disease slowly ravaging its core.

The postwar era represented an exceptional moment in the history of capitalism, characterised by unprecedented dynamism, wage rises, high productivity and relatively stable growth. For those who benefited from this dynamism – largely white male employees from the Global North – social democracy provided the security of a strong welfare state, while the Fordist economic regime, with its long-term and large-scale capital investments, created the stable growth and durability required for secure employment and a broad trade union movement. At the centre of this consensus was a newly hegemonic US, rising from the economic debris left by World War II. Its central position in terms of manufacturing and exports generated the initial vitality of the period, later boosted by complementary competition from the emerging German and Japanese economies.[27]

This period, however, was short-lived. From the mid-1960s onward, the variety of goods produced by the US, Japanese and German economies became increasingly homogenous. Overcapacity soon set in, starting the crisis of profitability and the ensuing 'secular stagnation' we are still experiencing today.[28] Saddled with an outdated, more expensive production process, US manufacturing was first to suffer. Then, by breaking up Bretton Woods and devaluing the dollar through a series of exchange rate adaptations, the US shifted the crisis first onto Germany and Japan and then onto the rest of Europe. Global stagnation in manufacturing quickly commenced, an economic torpor that has only become more persistent and pronounced in the decades since.

As overcapacity congealed into stagnation, so began the global process now widely referred to as deindustrialization.

With global competition reaching a saturation point, the decline in manufacturing commenced in the US and soon spread across most high-GDP economies. Between 1965 and 1973, US manufacturing profitability fell by 43.5 per cent, setting the stage for similarly dramatic profit losses in the other G7 economies.[29] Between 1970 and 2017, the overall number of workers employed in domestic manufacturing in the US, German, Italian and Japanese economies fell by around a third; in the French, by a half; and in the UK, by nearly two-thirds.[30] Now, this combined and uneven development toward deindustrialization – a long-term, asymmetrical and often contradictory process – is no longer simply the preserve of the overdeveloped North. Year-on-year manufacturing represents an ever smaller proportion of global GDP.[31]

In times past, crises of profitability like that of the 1970s represented a historically cyclical, necessary and temporary feature of the system, tending to signal that a particular business cycle or industrial paradigm had run its course; that productivity gains had pushed down prices across all competitors so that relative advantages were ever shrinking. Markets would become saturated with homogenous goods of a similar price and quality and, in an attempt to recreate itself, capital would will its own destruction, throwing ever more labour by the wayside. A growing surplus of unemployed and underemployed would then wait to be redeployed once investment moved from unprofitable to new and profitable industries.[32] As new innovations gained traction, labour was reemployed and the cycle started afresh on a grander scale. To offer one example: in early modern England, the agricultural sector reached capacity as labour-saving innovations drove down prices, saturated markets and then displaced workers and devalued capital, pushing labour out of the countryside and into the newly emerging cities.[33] These workers did not remain redundant for long and were soon taken up by the emerging textile industry. As the spinning jenny and power loom were introduced, productivity in textiles soared, cheapening goods, driving consumer demand and, in turn, stimulating demand for labour. But as competition among textile firms intensified, market saturation soon set in. The subsequent profitability crisis threw more workers out of the workplace, swelling the surplus population, which, again, was soon soaked up by the emerging industries of electricity and telecommunications, further expanding the system.

This dynamic of 'displacement, replacement, expansion', however crude, figures the historical rhythm of labour as it undergoes the turbulent transitions between economic cycles. Following the crisis of the 1970s though, this rhythm has been disrupted. Informal work, underemployment, wage stagnation, jobless recoveries, widespread precarity and a withered workers' movement are some of the many ominous symptoms that reveal a more terminal crisis of employment.

One common argument for why this has happened is that an ongoing lag between machines displacing workers and the subsequent reskilling is preventing the reabsorption of the displaced into new industries.[34] Those thrown out of routine manufacturing jobs have simply not gained the skills required to become, say, a programmer. There are good reasons to doubt this position.

One significant reason is that computers – unlike telecommunications, electricity and steam – have a general applicability, reducing the demand for labour across a far wider range of industries than previous technologies.[35] Marx predicted that over the course of capitalism technological innovations would become more universal in their application, consolidating labour as an ever more redundant aspect of the production process.[36] Locating the grim terminus of Marx's prediction in the present, many theorists of automation argue that high productivity innovations in computation, and now in AI, are pushing increasing numbers of workers to the economic margin.[37] Yet this picture is not quite right either. Unlike past industrial paradigms, computation and other digital developments have failed to facilitate the gains in productivity that previously served to soak up the surplus and facilitate the system's expansion. As the economist Robert Solow quipped: 'You can see the computer age everywhere but in the productivity statistics.'[38]

It appears that, to some degree, rather than reproducing capital on a larger scale, the system is instead reproducing labour surpluses on a larger scale. But this has less to do with automation taking jobs and more with, as Robert Brenner and many have since pointed out, the decline of manufacturing profits, which not only spelled the end of a model of growth but failed to produce a new one.[39] Thus, the explanation for the fall in labour demand, as Aaron Benanav notes,

is not rising productivity-growth rates, as the automation theorists claim, but inadequate output demand, due to the proliferation of industrial capacities across the world, an associated over-accumulation of capital, and a consequent downshift in rates of manufacturing expansion and economic growth overall. These remain the primary economic and social causes of the slack in the labour market that is wracking workers across the world.[40]

This has been intensified by the waves of proletarianization that have taken place since the 1970s. Only temporarily satisfying capital's need to expand, the growth of the global workforce has compelled the system to accommodate ever larger labour supplies at a time when there is increasingly little demand for it. To accommodate a global workforce suddenly inflated by the inclusion of formerly communist nations in the 1980s and 1990s, as well as of many nations of the decolonised South, the system needed to expand rather than shrink the job pool. But instead of job creation there has primarily been job relocation, whereby competition has driven a great deal of work once done in the North to the cheaper regions of the South. On top of this, many of the manufacturing jobs that had only recently appeared in countries like China and India have already fallen victim to deindustrialization.[41]

But while the jobs apocalypse repeatedly predicted throughout the computer age has not yet materialised, unemployment over the long term is incontrovertibly rising. During the postwar period, the UK and US presided over economies with around 2 per cent unemployment, with others maintaining as little as 1 per cent.[42] Since then, 5 per cent has become the target for the US and much of Western Europe, while the OECD average now hovers slightly above that target.[43] On average, after the 1970s, US unemployment rates have been closer to 7 per cent.[44] In the EU, between 1960 and 1990, unemployment rose from an average of 2 to 8 per cent, where, aside from cyclical spikes such as during the 2008 crisis, it has remained fairly stable.[45] This may yet change in the wake of the Covid-19 pandemic.

Of greater significance, however, is the huge global transfer of labour from manufacturing to 'services' – an overly capacious term that has become a kind of economic shorthand for any jobs that are outside of manufacturing or agriculture, including finance, retail, hospitality and care work.[46] Countries that have deindustrialized most rapidly – such as the UK and the US – have seen the most precipitous rise in service sector employment. As the value of UK manufacturing between 1970 and 2016 dropped from over 30 per cent of the economy to 10 per cent, services jumped from a little over 50 to 80 per cent.[47] A similar trend looms over the US economy. The arithmetic is as simple as it is forbidding; over this period, services came to represent nearly the entire value of both the UK and US economies.

Unlike manufacturing, service jobs tend to be what the economist William Baumol theorised as 'technologically stagnant'.[48] They resist the technical enhancement that produces the large productivity gains seen in, say, the automotive industry. This is because, as Jason E. Smith notes, 'low-skill' service tasks such as 'cleaning a room or watching a child require styles of spatial perception and calculation, manual and physical dexterity, not to mention an implicit understanding of norms like what "clean" or "safe" mean in a given situation, that have stymied attempts at mimicry by machines.'[49] For this reason, these jobs remain recalcitrant to the kinds of automation that have affected the manufacturing sector and, thus, remain relatively labour-intensive. Ever greater numbers have been forced into these low-productivity jobs, which do not grow at the rate of manufacturing and hence suffer from decreasing shares of labour income. This is why so many jobs in warehouses, taxi driving, hospitality and retail are low-paid, part-time or entail bogus 'self-employment' contracts. In turn, increased competition means increased desperation, allowing employers to lower standards across the board. Those left behind are forced to fill the roles of – or otherwise invent – a seemingly never-ending range of new and esoteric services, colonising an ever wider range of human activities: think hired friends and pet babysitters. In this sense, the term 'services' is perhaps a misnomer, hardly capturing the veritable cornucopia of miseries a stagnant system has in store for workers.

Subemployment

If the crisis of the 1970s set the groundwork for the flexible, service-centric labour market pioneered in the 1980s and 1990s, then the response to the 2008 financial crisis consolidated these changes into a fully-fledged order of 'subemployment'. Subemployment describes work that is highly temporary, casual and contingent, work that involves large amounts of unpaid labour, significant underemployment or high levels of in-work-poverty, or work that, more often than not, no longer guarantees a life any better than the most abject forms of unemployment. The collective result of a recovery forever delayed, subemployment describes a series of interrelated phenomena that solidified in the post-2008 period. The past decade has ushered in a period of economically woeful and politically dangerous precarity guarded against by most governments of the Global North since the late nineteenth century. Unlike then – when much of the world still relied on noncapitalist agriculture – the majority of the world today depends on a wage, and one that is waning. Consequently, the global landscape of labour is stretching into a vast and desolate hinterland of informality, temping, gigs and pseudowork, much of which – like workfare – is created simply for the sake of taming surplus populations. Though it is happening in uneven ways, many now find themselves in the strange nether region between employment and unemployment – waged and wageless life – that has blossomed amid the ruins of industrial growth.

While others have sought to understand similar phenomena through terms like 'precariat' and 'malemployment', I return to the term 'subemployment' – first used by liberal economists in the 1970s – which, unlike other terms, leverages the various ways in which employment and unemployment have become something less than themselves.[50] Drawing on the full semantic range of the prefix 'sub-' (*viz*, under, below, imperfectly, nearly and dominated) helps to synthesise a range of seemingly disparate but interconnected phenomena into a term that allows us to name the dire results of decreasing demand in a moment of slowing growth.

In the Global North, subemployment might include the UK's growing number of agency jobs, temp positions and zero-hour contracts. Such contracts mean that workers do a few hours here and there, not enough to qualify them for employment rights but enough to prevent them from claiming benefits and appearing in unemployment statistics – a situation so uncertain that workers are compelled to accept hours whenever offered. Similarly, the German government's 'mini job' scheme offers precarious work totalling around €450/month to workers who forgo the core benefits of more standard employment. Pushing workers out of the welfare system and into in-work-poverty, these arrangements often represent a situation worse than total joblessness.[51] In the so-called 'gig economy', for instance, workers are denied all the rights afforded an employee but given none of the freedoms of an independent contractor. They are promised freedom from human supervision but find themselves under the greater tyranny of oppressive algorithms. Much of this work is prone to low wages and volatile hours, making work across multiple platforms necessary for survival.

In the UK and many of its neighbour countries, forcing workers into such undesirable work required a radical transformation of the welfare system that has, among other punitive measures, made unemployment itself resemble an actual job. Though beginning under Tony Blair's New Labour, the transformation of unemployment into something like employment reaches its grim peak under the workfare state of David Cameron's coalition government. Unemployment now entails significant work, with so called welfare schemes obliging 'jobseekers' to undertake daily job searches, make regular visits to their local Jobcentre Plus, compose detailed reports of their efforts and attend self-help workshops provided by private firms. As Ivor Southwood drolly notes:

> Unemployment is turned into a pastiche of a job, complete with mock workplace, clocking in and out times, and managers to report to; and the jobseeking subject, having being brought under the punitive authority of a private agency, is correspondingly privatised, both threatened with withdrawal of welfare and force-fed the aspirational discourse.[52]

When jobseeking does not look like having a job it involves – somewhat perversely – having a job, only in this case a job for which the claimant is not paid. Under the auspices of Help to Work, the workfare brainchild of the former Department of Work and Pensions minister Iain Duncan Smith, claimants were forced as part of receiving their benefits to work for free for the likes of Tesco, Nandos and Boots as 'work experience'.[53]

This free labour is the epitome of subemployment, or what Leigh Claire La Berge has referred to as 'decommodified labour'.[54] Think here of the intern who works for the promise of pay at some later date; the unpaid research assistant; or the online influencer who sacrifices a wage for the prospect of exposure. Freely employed, labour ceases to be a commodity and becomes decommodified – labour without a price which continues to produce profit.[55] Usually, decommodification describes government bringing goods or services outside of market exchange and providing them for free, so that workers can secure their basic needs without having to work – the NHS being a prime example.[56] But now there is a grim inversion of this utopian impulse, where the wage relation itself is brought out of exchange, so that the worker receives precisely nothing, while the employer enjoys labour for free. Decommodified labour is thus neither employed nor unemployed, neither inside nor outside the wage – the relation par excellence for a moment of rising surpluses, when the wage is increasingly missing but still structures our lives.[57]

As the overhaul of welfare under the Cameron government demonstrates, decommodified labour is often made available to capital with the state's assistance. Rising numbers entering state workfare programmes in countries such as the US, Australia, Hungary and Singapore reveal a world in which not finding a job can mean being forced to work for free at the state's discretion. And where unemployment is not deemed punishable by workfare it is judged to be an actual crime. In her book on California's prison system, *Golden Gulag*, Ruth Wilson Gilmore shows how incarceration expanded as unemployment rose in the latter half of the twentieth century into a vast industrial complex for turning surplus into productive populations, a process that has only further consolidated itself across much of the world after 2008.[58] Growing numbers of inmates are compelled to encounter their disposability in the most brutal fashion; forcibly 'contracted' as firefighters to hold the line against the deadly wildfires in northern California, or to operate dangerously outdated machinery under the threatening gaze of armed guards.[59]

Though microwork feeds off the whole range of phenomena that characterise subemployment in the Global North – precarity, underemployment, unwaged work, forced labour and high levels of algorithmic automation – the majority of those who power platforms were forged long before the 2008 crisis in that great laboratory of subemployment: the vast and expanding informal sector of the Global South. Relieved of the mercy of the colonies, then thrown to the mercy of stagnant markets and structural adjustment, many countries from the South have seen formal employment extended only to a privileged minority. In the decade following the 2008 crash, informal employment came to represent 68 per cent of the labour market in Asia and the Pacific, 85 per cent in Africa and 40 per cent in the Arab states.[60] Amid this 'structural dearth of formal jobs... transformed into an overwhelming spectacle of informal competition', a lumpen mass of economic castoffs undertakes a disorienting array of roles – hawking goods, selling services and hunting for errands.[61] This does not represent the unquenchable spirit of entrepreneurialism, as often argued by representatives of the Washington Consensus, but a living exhibition of human misery. The term 'self-employment' is stretched to excruciating semantic proportions by the grizzly parades of brutality that take the form of hand-drawn rickshaw drivers and illegal organ donors. A shadow economy of 'wage hunters and gatherers' continually searching for bits and pieces of work, the informal sector is less the scraps flung from the capitalist table, more the fallen detritus, skilfully hoovered up by those who have never been thrown a morsel.[62]

Though the idea that informality is hermetically sealed off from the economy proper has always been more pertinent to the likes of the World Bank than to actual lived experience, the distinction appears ever flimsier as micro-tasks and gigs proliferate in place of full-time employment. As Mike Davis notes, 'part of the informal proletariat, to be sure, is a stealth workforce for the formal economy.'[63] Though for the most part a minor phenomenon, the means by which companies like Walmart extend their supply chains to India's hawkers is well documented, as is the global fashion industry's use of the kirana clothes stores that line the streets of Mumbai and Delhi.[64] But what was once peripheral now comes to the core. Through the more extensive and thus less traceable supply chains achieved via microwork sites, platform capitalism brings both the logic and realities of informality to the very heart of accumulation as a new norm. All of the largest companies in the world are today powered by a covert crowd of the system's castoffs. Platforms have found amid those struggling to stay afloat in informal work – or else barely clinging onto a life in formal employment – a desperate mass to be tempted with the promise of a better life. Such a promise, however, is broken as soon as it is made; the petty services of the informal sector resemble little more than a blueprint for the microtasks of big tech, with neither offering anything in the way of rights, routine, role, security or a future. That both tissue sellers and data labellers receive the World Bank's appellation of 'microentrepreneur' reveals an inconvenient truth: that the vast hinterland stretching from microwork to street hawking is divided only by a modicum of legal recognition.[65]

2

Artificial or Human Intelligence?

For platform tycoons, the ambiguous status of microworkers is not so much legal as ontological. Notoriously, Jeff Bezos describes the workers of Amazon Mechanical Turk as 'artificial artificial intelligence'. The original Mechanical Turk was an eighteenth-century device created by the Hungarian inventor Johann Wolfgang Ritter von Kempelen. Designed to resemble a chess-playing automaton, the device, in fact, was no such thing. The Mechanical Turk – a puppet dressed in orientalist garb – concealed under its fez and robes a human chess master. After seeing the device on one of its many tours around the US by showman Johann Maelzel, the less-than-dazzled poet Edgar Allan Poe was so convinced of its fraudulence that he wrote an exposé, 'Maelzel's Chess Player', to draw attention to the hoax. A predetermined mechanism beating a spontaneous human mind at chess was impossible, Poe claimed, for 'no one move in chess necessarily follows upon any one other. From no particular disposition of the men at one period of a game can we predicate their disposition at a different period'.[1]

With the advent of machine learning and of computers capable of making just such predictions, one might assume that such naive illusions are behind us. After all, computers now exist that can beat any human at chess. Yet there remain a great many seemingly simple tasks that machines still struggle to complete. For these tasks, Bezos – no less a confidence man than Maelzel – devised a platform named after Kempelen's Mechanical Turk. In a postmodern twist on the eighteenth-century device, the platform disguises humans as computation, now to woo a credulous – or simply cynical – audience of start-ups, conglomerates and university researchers.

Mechanical Turk began life as a service only available to programmers employed by Amazon. Back in 2001, during the heady days of the dot-com bubble, long before AI became the lucrative market it is today, Amazon created the site to solve a simple in-house problem: its algorithms were failing to recognise many duplicate product listings. Realising the tasks could be more efficiently completed by workers, Amazon decided to patent 'a hybrid machine/human computing arrangement', namely, Mechanical Turk. Via an application programming interface (API), Mechanical Turk gave the company's programmers the ability to write software that automatically outsourced to workers tasks too complex for computers.

Recognising a growing demand for cheap labour across a still nascent platform economy, Amazon publicly launched Mechanical Turk in 2005. The site's now familiar role – hosting contractors who post 'human intelligence tasks' (HITs) to precarious workers – offered a prototype for the sites that followed. Premised on the extraordinary growth of artificial intelligence over the last decade, Appen, Playment and Clickworker now host millions of workers worldwide. Until fully automated solutions arrive for petty data problems, these numbers will continue to grow. Estimating precisely by how much remains difficult, due to the challenge of measuring the future of AI growth. One conservative estimate suggests that the AI market worldwide was worth around $10 billion in 2018 and will be worth around $126 billion in 2022.[2]

Like the expansion of the service sector described in the previous chapter, the growth of AI is the result of a capitalist system adapting to decline in perverse ways, turning to what was once an economic by-product in an attempt to reinvigorate economic growth. The commodification of data, once regarded as an externality, is now central to the business strategies of all the world's largest companies, not just the big tech platforms like Google, Amazon, Alibaba and Facebook, but also many banks and supermarkets. An immense infrastructure of extraction, processing and analysis has led to exponential advances in data technology and computation.[3] The mutually reinforcing factors of unrestricted venture capital, sophisticated algorithms, Moore's law and 'Big Data' have accelerated the machine learning advances behind innovations as diverse as autonomous vehicles, cloud computing, smart assistants and advertising strategies, as well as methods for filtering and recommending video content.

Though the terms 'AI' and 'machine learning' are often used interchangeably, machine learning is actually a particular school of AI development. It relies on large data sets to train models which are then used to make further predictions. Integrated into this process are algorithms that analyse data to extract patterns and make predictions, and then use those predictions to generate further algorithms. In learning and creating new rules, these products develop in ways ostensibly resembling human intelligence. Of those technologies currently available, artificial neural networks (ANNs), closely modelled on the brain's neuron connections, are the most sophisticated and widely used. In a process known as 'training', the neural network is repeatedly exposed to instances of a specific data object, an image of a cat or an audio clip of a melody, perhaps, and then the weighted interplay of the network's various layers is manipulated by an algorithm until the network is able to recognise the object. This new data then feeds back automatically into the network, creating a more sophisticated algorithm.

The richer the data these technologies are exposed to, the more comprehensive their training and the more sophisticated their capacities become, enhancing their performance in tasks as varied as image categorisation, text classification and speech recognition. In many areas, such developments have bestowed machines with capacities that frequently match or surpass those of humans. Deep learning algorithms are able to translate sentences with such a degree of sensitivity to context and nuance that they often exceed the abilities of human translators. AI diagnosticians are already at least as proficient as doctors at identifying certain types of cancer; and speech recognition technologies are predicted to replace many workers in call centres and fast-food restaurants in the next two decades.[4]

The speed at which these technologies have developed has led some to worry that as much as half of the world's work – predominantly in the service sector – is at risk of automation by 2030.[5] Because services has reabsorbed all the labour thrown off by manufacturing, and because no other sector has materialised in the meantime, such a situation would leave vast swathes of the population with nowhere to go.[6]

To support their claims, automation doomsayers tend to point at specific innovations already in use. In call centres, the familiar voice at the end of the line explaining 'Your call may be recorded for training purposes' now also means the call is being recorded for machine learning purposes.[7] McDonalds has acquired the AI start-up Apprente in a plan to replace the voice of humans at drive-through windows with the automated speech of chatbots. In the retail sector, staff-less, automated retail outlets are popping up in many countries, including the UK, the US and Sweden. Stores like Amazon Go, euphemistically termed 'just-walk-out shopping', have combined automatic scanning and mobile apps with facial recognition that matches customer faces to the items in their bag. The threat posed by autonomous vehicles to taxi drivers has in recent years become a major flashpoint. While successful trials of self-driving taxis have taken place in London, Singapore and New York, the vehicles have been deployed in many other sectors too.[8] Cargo-handling vehicles, hauling trucks, agricultural vehicles and delivery robots have all been used widely across contexts such as hospitals, factories, farming and mining. 'High-skill' services like finance have undergone significant automation from the early 1980s, a process that since the 2008 crisis has accelerated rapidly. In 2000, the Goldman Sachs equity trading desk had six hundred employees; by 2016, all but two had been replaced by AI-powered trading algorithms.[9]

Grave forecasts that such technologies will eventually be implemented on a far wider scale forget that a particular technology is generalised only if it turns out to be cheaper than employing a workforce. Some now counter that the low wages that have offered a dubious protection to workers over the last forty years may no longer be enough to hold back the tide. The growing risks of cataclysmic weather events and pandemics may mean that workers soon represent a greater cost to firms than robots. The Covid-19 pandemic has displayed just how volatile labour power can be as a source of profit for capital, with many workers across the world forced out of their jobs, sometimes for lengthy periods, by lockdown or disease.[10] Many firms undoubtedly worry that coronavirus is only the prologue to an age of zoonotic disease. While some worry, others seem almost jubilant that as natural barriers to zoonotic spillover are further collapsed, capital creates a contradiction to which it must respond by expediting the transfer of economic activity from labour to machine. As Anuja Sonalker, CEO of Steer Tech, states, 'Humans are biohazards, machines are not.'[11]

Whether catastrophic event or disruptive innovation, concerns about a grand annihilation of workers by machines are nearly always speculative. For this reason, many have challenged what they consider to be an overly apocalyptic consensus. Astra Taylor, in her essay 'The Automation Charade', implores us to 'reckon with the ideology of automation, and its attendant myth of human obsolescence'.[12] We should be wary of 'fauxtomation', a kind of automation illusion, exemplified by the figure of the Mechanical Turk worker.[13] In a more circumspect tone, Aaron Benanav acknowledges that advanced robotics and artificial intelligence are here, but they are yet to cause the levels of 'job destruction' forecast by automation prophets.[14]

At least some of the dispute stems from the fact that a good working definition of automation across historical contexts is hard to come by. Quoting the novelist Kurt Vonnegut, Benanav asserts that 'true automation takes place whenever an entire "job classification has been eliminated. Poof."'[15] This somewhat reductive gloss typifies standard accounts of automation.

Today, however, the impact of automation has less to do with the erasure of whole jobs and more to do with adaptations to a given job's task composition and, subsequently, the overall quality of the work. Most jobs are the result of various tasks with varying degrees of susceptibility to automation. Automation might not wipe out a whole job, just some of the tasks that comprise it.

In this spirit, AI does not tend to create fully automated systems but rather systems that partially automate jobs and outsource certain tasks to the crowd.

As sites like Mechanical Turk suggest, the automation of some service work is perhaps never likely to result in full mechanization, but rather in machine-human hybridity. In work which has historically proven difficult to automate, machine learning squeezes out small productivity gains in terms of the partial automation of specific tasks and managerial functions, the hyperdivision of labour and just-in-time outsourcing. Where certain tasks are automated, other once geographically tethered tasks are set free to wander the globe in search of opportunities for labour arbitrage. Subsequently, work once properly waged is not only proletarianized but by default informalized, parcelled into badly paid, erratic piecework, and torn from the regulatory frameworks that legislate pay and rights. Not bound to any given jurisdiction, microwork sites unpick the legal ties between worker, employer and place. As Jamie Woodcock and Mark Graham note, 'A small business in New York can hire a freelance transcriber in Nairobi one day and New Delhi the next. No offices or factories need to be built, no local regulations are adhered to, and – in most cases – no local taxes are paid.'[16]

In another more obvious sense, microwork sites stage an ever more intimate partnering of low-skill service work and automated systems. Microwork teaches, modulates and corrects AI and, in doing so, shows it how to fulfill the role of labour, even if some of these technologies never come to pass as general conditions of the capitalist economy. For the autonomous vehicle to avoid accidents, the chatbot to comprehend cues and the automatic trader to take sensible risks relies first on machine learning being trained on clean, annotated data; then, once up and running, continual supervision by workers. Unless refined, data threatens to train an algorithm in ways that contravene the programmer's intent. To take one example, chatbots are trained on limited, annotated data to recognise specific words and grammar, but when left to unlimited data they tend to act erratically. To recognise specific words an algorithm is exposed repeatedly to either audio or text, sometimes thousands of times over. For bots used in commerce, this data is supplied by workers on microwork sites like Appen, who feed the bot exact text or record themselves speaking specific words or sentences.[17] But when let loose on large amounts of raw data, chatbots gravitate – as algorithms so often do – toward extreme content. Microsoft's Tay, a 'playful' conversation bot, was given free rein to learn from Twitter content. Twenty-four hours later, Tay was tweeting comments eerily reminiscent of those of Donald Trump: '@ godblessameriga WE'RE GOING TO BUILD A WALL AND MEXICO IS GOING TO PAY FOR IT'.[18] Algorithms do unexpected things – like repeat protofascist edicts – when training happens unsupervised, without the legions of workers on Appen or Mechanical Turk to first refine the data.

Once data has been cleaned and annotated, algorithms still rely on a variety of human inputs to help train, calibrate and correct their operations. Twitter, for instance, often uses workers on Mechanical Turk to quickly identify trending queries, analyse their content and feed them back into its real-time search. When the query 'Big Bird' started trending after a comment made by Mitt Romney during the 2012 presidential debates, workers on Mechanical Turk were asked to quickly determine which users were actually searching for tweets related to Sesame Street.[19] Such events rely on a workforce to make decisions swiftly and save the algorithm from making costly errors – errors that would impact Twitter's ability to extract useful data and predict user preferences. The decisions made by workers are then used as training for the algorithm so that its chances of completing the task are better next time.

This is not just the case with online work but also jobs that take place in physical space. On the Berkeley campus, food-delivery robots are partly controlled by a remote workforce in Colombia paid $2/hour, who take control and steer the automated bots when they make mistakes.[20] If we imagine the automation of services in this way – a process of ongoing human supervision and correction

– the question is no longer one of absolute superfluity but relative superfluity: just how much are workers involved and to what extent can they make a living? Microwork exemplifies the way that AI tends to informalize rather than fully automate work. It betokens a future in which growing numbers of workers are not erased by machines but squeezed to the point of vanishing.

From Lumpen to Curated Data Work

While work continues beyond work's apocalyptic end, for a growing number the coup de grâce is instead a slow death by poverty-pay tasks. That a growing amount of this barely subsistence work takes place online represents a development unique to platform capitalism. But the division of data work into small tasks is itself not new. As Lily Irani notes:

> A 1985 case, Donovan vs DialAmerica, tells of an earlier version of [Mechanical Turk]–style labor. An employer sent cards with names to home workers hired as independent contractors. These contractors had to ascertain the correct phone number for each name; they were paid per task.[21]

While these workers were eventually determined by courts to be employees entitled under the Fair Labor Standards Act to a minimum wage, today's digital pieceworkers are not so lucky. And unlike these sporadic instances of home-based data work, online microwork represents an increasingly competitive large-scale industry. Scale, Hive, Appen and Lionsbridge are used by a whole range of big tech clients – as well as banks and supermarkets.

The industry can be split into two basic types: curated crowd and crude crowd sites. Exemplary of the latter, Mechanical Turk is open to any worker or requester, provides a multitude of general online services and consistently pays below subsistence wages.[22] The most lumpen of online piecework, Human Intelligence Tasks (HITs) can be anything from surveys, short translation tasks or image and audio classification to the verification of decisions already made by algorithms. Often paid no more than cents and prey to a 20 per cent cut from Mechanical Turk, HITs offer a weatherglass onto a system that no longer even pretends that workers are anything more than disposable life. Other platforms included in this category are the massive German company Clickworker, which operates in over 130 countries with over 2 million workers, the vast Chinese crowdwork site Zhubajie and the lesser-known platform Microworkers.

The more stringently regulated and specialist platforms offer curated crowd services.[23] These are customised machine learning services tailored to specific, often long-term clients. Scale, for instance, sources workers to process data for warehouse robotics. Lionsbridge supports a wide range of natural language processing projects, including automatic speech recognition, sentiment analysis and chatbot training data. The largest of these sites, Appen, supports machine learning across financial services, retail, healthcare and the automotive industry, and partners with Amazon Web Services, Microsoft and Google Cloud on a range of projects. Though not the largest in terms of users, Appen is now one of few microwork sites to become a publicly traded company, and it is using its increasing power as a multinational to buy up smaller start-ups such as Leapforce and Figure Eight.[24]

Attuned to the finer points of machine learning training, work on these sites often arrives as packages containing similar tasks, which can last for an hour or sometimes as long as a day, and which often pay somewhat more than tasks on crude crowd sites. For instance, task packages used to train facial recognition technology are based on a series of data subsets, including faces in particular poses, in make-up or masks, faces occluded by poor lighting or in the distance and faces expressing different emotions. Because tasks on these sites often require significant skill or a particular area of expertise, access often depends on assessments of language and technology skills, as well as wider cultural dexterity. Lionsbridge, for instance, claims to leverage a crowd of 500,000 linguistic experts such as translators.[25] Common across both curated and crude crowd sites, this repackaging of once prestigious, well-paid employment as 'low-skill' tasks displays in stark terms capital's violent path through the 'vocations', turning professionals into proletariats.

Many larger tech companies also have their own internal platforms. These tend to attract workers through crude or curated sites. Microsoft's Universal Human Relevance System (UHRS) was created to respond spontaneously to the company's immediate needs, something to which external platforms like Appen and Lionsbridge are not suited. Uber acquired Mighty AI for similar reasons and uses it to process the large amounts of data extracted from its drivers in order to develop autonomous vehicles. Google created Raterhub to contract 'raters' – workers, usually from the Philippines – to assess how well the company's search results meet user expectations: whether the results are of good quality, and whether the content is illegal, pornographic or offensive. The data produced is used to show Google's algorithms how to complete these tasks automatically. The pay is pitiful, the hours long and the job psychologically hazardous.[26] Holocaust denial, child pornography and violent terrorist imagery are just some of the traumatic content a worker might encounter when rating or moderating.

Though the terms 'crude' and 'curated' allow us to distinguish two general types, there is in fact a significant amount of crossover in terms of the services each offers.

Mechanical Turk is regularly used for rudimentary purposes – by academics to source cheap interviewees and marketing firms to fill surveys. But the platform is also used for more specialised projects, such as training the facial recognition software of Amazon and the real-time search functions of Twitter.[27] Training often entails levels of cultural dexterity associated with salaried white-collar work but garners a fraction of the pay and none of the rights and benefits. As demonstrated by the example of workers showing Twitter's algorithms how to identify tweets relating to Big Bird, making such decisions swiftly and correctly – work essential to Twitter's prediction of user preferences – requires a near Zeitgeist-level of knowledge surrounding contemporary events. Only twenty years ago, equivalent cultural work would have garnered a full-time job with wages. Now, for little to no pay, it goes to an overeducated surplus, who may have a university-level education and the skills and training for professional work but nowhere to employ them.

This stripping of pay, rights and skills represents the real and present impact that automation is having on the service sector. Yet, the concrete experience of workers is often lost amid sensational speculations of unprecedented job loss. Whether naysayer or doomsayer, automation theorists tend to focus debate on mass unemployment. But the jobless armageddon is a red herring. Instead, we are seeing ever more service jobs transformed into gig-, micro- and crowdwork, where working on and alongside the algorithm is the form automation tends to take. In the case of microwork, these 'jobs' too often resemble joblessness.

3

Humans-as-a-Service

Among microwork's boosters and reluctant advocates, there is a tendency to accentuate its novelty as a new source of waged employment. There is a sense that AI may not, after all, be the job killer many supposed but a job creator. The World Bank has spearheaded this vanguard of dangerous optimism, pushing microwork as the solution to the woes of the world's poorest and most marginalized. A longtime advocate of labour arbitrage, the World Bank advises, 'low labour cost gives a competitive advantage to workers from developing countries.'[1] In tones so flat they sound nearly ironic, such statements exemplify a dire new consensus on global development. As the title of a book by Leilah Janah, late CEO of Samasource, suggests, the aim is now to 'Give Work', not aid.[2] In an effort to entice the NGO and state wardens of such labour, a further briefing titled 'Game-Changing Opportunities for Youth Employment in the Middle East and North Africa' makes the entirely dubious claim that the average US microworker makes up to $40,000 per annum.[3] In a similarly meretricious vein, the *Harvard Business Review* boldly asserts that microwork offers a 'living wage' and 'skills' to the otherwise jobless.[4] As if blind to any sense of contradiction, it then goes on to assert that 'customers, by using microwork centres instead of large for-profit vendors, can get jobs done for 30 per cent to 40 per cent less'. A living wage, indeed.

Even the responses of less ardently neoliberal institutions such as the International Labour Organization (ILO) have ranged from gentle boosterism to total quietism. In a large-scale survey of microworkers conducted by the ILO, the authors admit that the conditions of online data work are far from perfect but remain at pains to emphasise the 'new opportunities for workers to earn income'.[5] The same problems exist among much academic literature on the subject. Mary L. Gray and Siddharth Suri's *Ghost Work,* an often clear-sighted account of the perils such workers face, at times too readily follows the fictions pushed by microwork boosters. Drawing on the first-hand accounts of actual workers, the book reveals the motivations that drive people toward online tasks, such as the chance of gaining skills and a better job.[6] A more honest portrayal of such work would need to emphasise that there is little evidence that such aspirations are ever actually met. By the scant evidence the authors do offer, microwork appears more as a mirage in the desert of current employment than an oasis of opportunity.

If this book has one aim it is to show that microwork is not a new source of jobs and skills, but something akin to the grizzly spectacles of survival one might find on the streets of Victorian England, nineteenth-century Naples or modern Mumbai. Beyond the hackneyed bootstrap dogma of institutions like the World Bank, we should ask: what does the wage actually look like on microwork sites? Does the work offer the skills and benefits of an actual occupation? Do these conditions differ from other forms of wageless survivalism? And do they prevent the kinds of organisation and unity once seen in the traditional working class? Such an enquiry can help to guide us toward new kinds of resistance in a moment when work again feels obscure yet, somehow, bewilderingly familiar.

From Wage to Wager

What if work meant play and working hard meant hardly working at all? This is the promise made by platforms such as Playment and Clickworker. Adorned with images of hip, young people relaxing on sofas idly browsing laptops, their sites suggest that if work still exists in our brave new economy, it's no less fun than playing a videogame or shopping for clothes. A sepia-toned snapshot of the remote work dream, as alluring as it is mendacious, gives lumpen piecework a glint of aspiration and glamour. As if even the mention of 'work' or 'workers' might upset this gentle air of bonhomie, the sites refer only to 'users', 'taskers' and 'players'. Play now equals pay. 'Brightly gamified compliance regimes' extend to the work process itself.[7] On-screen rankings, nonmonetary rewards and access to new levels of accreditation – such as Mechanical Turk's enigmatic 'Masters qualification' – are used to gamify tasks in ways that blur the boundaries between work and play.

But when wages become 'tokens' or 'rewards', leisure and ease soon look more like theft than fun. Linguistic flourishes such as 'reward' hint at the fact that tasks represent a gamble, the wage less a contract and more a wager made by the worker when deciding to accept a task.[8] And when not paid below subsistence levels – 90 per cent of tasks on Mechanical Turk pay less than $0.10 per task – they do not pay at all.[9] One of the largest surveys carried out across microwork sites found that 30 per cent of workers regularly go unpaid.[10] On Clickworker as much as 15 per cent of all tasks go unpaid.[11] In other words, capital's online infrastructure runs to a significant degree on unpaid labour. This continues a longer trajectory, as Melinda Cooper notes: 'Under post-Fordist conditions, the wage itself has become something of a speculative proposition... conditional on the

45

achievement of performance indicators' and 'unspecified hours of unpaid work readiness.'[12] The worker thus operates increasingly in a quasi-magical economy of gambling and lottery. Microwork represents the grim apex of this trajectory, where the possibility of the next task being paid tempts workers time and again to return for more. Intricate reward schedules and contestable pricing gamify tasks and effectively repackage superfluity and precarity as new, exciting forms of work-cum-leisure.

When wage becomes wager, the status of the worker itself is brought into question. Wage and work are bound together as one under capital. This is not only of ontological interest; it has a vital political valence, for the coherence between worker and wage is the ground from which so much struggle against capital has emerged. Without a wage, one is not quite a worker but a slave, or else surplus – categories that are conceptually and, by extension, politically distinct. It is for this reason that campaigns like Wages For Housework have demanded a wage be extended 'behind the hidden abode' to domestic labour.[13] As Sylvia Federici notes: 'The unwaged condition of housework has been the most powerful weapon in reinforcing the common assumption that *housework is not work*.'[14] That the wage so often goes missing in the case of microwork reveals a similar denial of 'worker' status, a reminder that, as with care and domestic work, petty data tasks do not deserve formal recognition.

Microwork sites do of course promise pay, but because they give requesters carte blanche to act as they wish, vast numbers of tasks go unpaid. Structures that appear neutral are in fact often organised around systematic efforts to make the wage optional as opposed to obligatory. Even when paid, tasks are priced at such abysmally low rates that wages shed their reproductive function. On Mechanical Turk, the only platform where wages have been calculated, workers make less than $2 per hour.[15]

Of the many ways these sites facilitate wage theft, the most effective is the form of payment itself. Looking past the shiny pomp of autonomous vehicles and delivery drones, one sees that among Silicon Valley's most dazzling labour-saving devices is a throwback to nineteenth-century economy. Piece rates, which let employers pay by the finished product, are more than other forms of payment at eminent risk of wage theft. Let us not forget that it is for this very reason that Marx saw piece rates as 'the form of wage most appropriate to the capitalist mode of production'.[16] A common feature of the Victorian model of capitalism, piece rates all but vanished in the Global North with twentieth-century rationalization processes, which allowed tasks to be standardized and wages paid hourly. But they have remained the most common form of payment across the South's gargantuan informal sector, a false lifeline to those forced to eke out a living at the system's margin: rickshaw pullers and waste pickers, as well as the sweatshop workers who are subcontracted to work for domestic or global supply chains.

The return of piece rates to the US and Europe is premised on a crude solution to the service sector productivity puzzle. Without an easy automation solution to jobs like food, postal delivery and accountancy, sites like Deliveroo and Upwork have kindly reimagined Victorian capitalism for professional and precariat alike, introducing piece-work across a range of once waged or salaried professions to push workers to merciless levels of intensity. This is no more the case than with sites like Mechanical Turk, where rigorous standards of quality are often of less importance than brute speed. AI can already do many tasks listed on microwork sites, but workers maintain the upper hand when it comes to pace.[17] Given that a five-minute HIT (Human Intelligence Task) on Mechanical Turk can be paid as little as 20 cents, workers must work quickly simply to meet their daily needs.

47

With tasks paid by the piece, workers experience long fallow periods as they search for new jobs, which often means longer hours to make ends meet. Like others made fugitive to the market, more time is spent hunting for jobs than actually completing them. A Mechanical Turk worker from a former Mining town in Appalachia describes a typical day on the platform:

> If I work 12–16 hours a day, I'll make maybe $5/hour. That's when there is work, but when you're sitting in between jobs and you consider that time, when you're just looking for work, then the hourly wage falls dramatically. There are so many of us now, and fewer quality jobs. Sometimes I wake up in the middle of the night just to see if I can grab some good requests. Most HITs are gone if you don't click right away.[18]

As with other sections of the informal economy, microwork sites stage a 'chronic super abundance of labour'.[19] This oversupply and a lack of employment options elsewhere compels workers to spend their nights hunting for tasks paying little more than a few cents. Unlike the spontaneous surpluses swamping cities like Mumbai and Kinshasa, such abundance in the digital realm is strategically planned. Microwork sites are organised to attract greater numbers of workers than there are tasks available, to ramp up productivity and drive down wages, meaning all must accept poor conditions such as long hours and working through the night. Accounts such as the one above are not uncommon. A large study on microwork in Sub-Saharan Africa found Kenyan workers regularly putting in 78-hour weeks.[20]

Under the pressure of accelerated pace and ever longer working hours, accuracy tends to suffer. Yet, with tasks paid so little, mistakes are of little concern to requesters, who distribute vast numbers of similar tasks to multiple workers with the knowledge that a great many 'finished products' will be unusable. All that matters to requesters is that enough passably decent tasks are fulfilled in a short time frame.

To make sure pace is maintained, most sites allow requesters to place specific time limits on tasks, which, if broken, result in docked pay. On Leapforce (acquired by Appen in 2017), a typical task was limited to anything between thirty seconds and fifteen minutes, often outsourced from the site's largest client – Google Raterhub.[21] Yet, despite hosting such reputable clients, Leapforce's platform was clunky and would frequently lag.[22] Oftentimes a task would take more time to load than the time allotted to complete it. One can see the problem here: the requester – in this case, Google – still receives the completed task but can lawfully retract payment due to delayed completion. Even on sites more sophisticated than Leapforce, workers remain susceptible to the caprices of server volatility, poor connectivity and hostile requesters. On Mechanical Turk, time restrictions are only indicators of how long a task should take, but because the restrictions are defined by requesters, who are eager to cut costs, a task might be marketed as one dollar for fifteen minutes but actually take closer to thirty to complete, a reality that a worker might remain unaware of until they are ten minutes into the task. Once under way, backing out means surrendering payment.

Even tasks completed in the allotted time frame frequently go unpaid. Those deemed 'bad quality' by requesters are more often than not simply rejected out of hand. In their study of Amazon Mechanical Turk's payment system, M. Six Silberman and Lilly Irani found that

> a photo tagging task might be posted twice for two workers
> to complete. If the two workers produce the same answers,
> the requester's software can pay both workers. If they

49

produce different answers, the software can post the task a third time... In this workflow, the workers in the 'majority' are paid; the 'dissenter' is assumed to be incorrect and is not paid.[23]

In this specific case, only one out of three workers loses their wages. But this might happen on a far larger scale with hundreds of workers completing the same tasks – say, with sixty workers paid, thirty unpaid. Because the requester can easily claim that any finished task is unsatisfactory – no matter how low their standards may actually be – and subsequently withhold payment, the system readily blurs the boundaries between paid and unpaid labour, commodification and decommodification.

The sweating system, then, returns with a vengeance, with digital sweatshops far better suited to wage theft than their Victorian counterparts. Delphic software architectures turn a quantitative change in the amount of wage theft into a qualitative shift, whereby daylight robbery, now on a systemic scale, pushes the wage to its farcical conclusion as a discretionary reward. In a nineteenth-century textile workshop, a certain amount of reliability regarding who pays the wages, as well as where and when, meant that workers could at least identify a thief – a necessary step to taking strike or legal action. Even today, rates are usually paid by a single, often familiar employer, a relatively easy target for worker pushback – think here of the 1934 general strike of US textile workers, who fought against diminished piece rates by walking out.[24] On microwork sites, there are no workplaces. 'Employers' are multiple over the course of a single day and remain entirely anonymous – hidden behind opaque interfaces – leaving the worker with no idea whom they are working for.

So-called 'bad' requesters would not be able to refuse payment if platforms were not organised so as to encourage infringements of the wage contract. To protect their status as intermediaries, platforms operate under the guise of 'neutrality' and refuse to enter disputes between workers and requesters. The partisan neutrality of free-market doctrine is here ramped up to absurd levels of prejudice – a neutrality that allows requesters to withdraw wages for unusable tasks, yet still grants requesters full intellectual property rights; that offers requesters total anonymity but makes details about workers publicly known; that allows requesters to come and go as they please but traps workers via payment holding periods. Curated crowd sites like Appen and Lionsbridge attract long-term clients, but these clients are under no obligation to remain on the platform. This means requesters can easily vanish without paying, while workers are forced to wait until they can cash in their wages, sometimes for as long as thirty days after joining the site or until their payment balance reaches a specific sum.[25]

This frequently means wages disappear before the worker has a chance to withdraw them. One of the more draconian measures taken by microwork sites is to shut down the accounts of those who protest or act in ways deemed to undermine a site's rules, often without so much as a word from the platform, which can mean all wages stored during the holding period are lost.[26] Expulsion from the platform more often than not is the result of more innocent activity – whether glitches in the software or so-called 'errors' on the part of the worker, such as changing address or bank details – often seen as red flags for malfeasance.[27]

The story of capitalism is, in no small part, the story of individuals gradually coming to terms with the disciplinary framework of waged life, even as gainful work itself is eroded. As E. P. Thompson notes, 'in all these ways – by the division of labour; the supervision of labour; fines; bells and clocks; money incentives; preachings

and schoolings; the suppression of fairs and sports –
new labour habits were formed.'[28] To these techniques,
intended to forge habits conducive to orderly labour, we
may now add account closures and public score systems.
Effectively allowing 'employers' to sack workers without
so much as a warning, they return the world of work to
a place that resembles Victorian England, only now with
the objective pretences of algorithmic decision-making.

Score systems offer a veneer of objectivity, allowing
requesters to numerically measure worker performance.
But they are in their own way as partisan as account
closures. How they are handled differs from platform to
platform, though they tend to entail each worker receiving
an aggregate score of ratings previously given by requesters, made public on the site so that other requesters can
identify good or potentially bad performers. A rare few
ascend the ranks to the heady heights of Master rating
and the better paid tasks such ratings bring. For most,
however, there is only paralysis or a downward stair-
case on which workers can only watch as their ratings
decline. Metrics thus take on a near tyrannical quality,
often representing the difference between finding work
again and disenfranchisement. On the site Microworkers,
an approval rating ('temporary success rate') that drops
below 75 per cent prevents access to jobs for up to thirty
days.[29] As this example shows, if a worker's ratings suffer
at the hands of a particularly strict or hostile requester
their reputation plunges and opportunities to find more
work shrink.

A whole architecture thus exists to divest the wage of
its already tenuous contractual status, granting the likes
of Google and Microsoft excessive powers of anonymity and mobility, allowing them to withhold payment for
tasks that fail to meet unreasonable time limits, while
effectively making workers inert, transparent and, in
many respects, powerless to protest.

Alongside these stealth tactics are cruder forms of wage debasement. Many platforms, for instance, pay exclusively in nonmonetary 'rewards'. On Picoworkers, wages become Amazon gift cards and cryptocurrency; on Swagbucks, Walmart coupons and Starbucks vouchers; and on InstaGC, the worker chooses between a variety of gift cards for high street brands. In an interview, a founder of Crowdflower casually revealed that the company 'paid workers in points for various online reward programs and videogame credits.'[30] While vouchers and tokens are technically commodities (so avoid the total decommodification of payment) they can hardly be described as money. There are good reasons why the wage comes in monetary form. Money, as the numéraire of the capitalist system, is exchangeable for all other commodities. And while Amazon may claim to be the 'Everything Store' – a kind of universal equivalent in corporate form – its gift cards are not as universal as the dollar.[31] A voucher restricts the realm of exchange to the products or services sold by a specific firm and therefore reduces the means by which a worker's daily needs can be met. One cannot live off Starbucks alone.

Mechanical Turk is perhaps the most interesting in this respect, considering its size and geographical scope. Workers from across the world use the platform, but only a limited number have access to payments via bank transfer. The majority, in the words of Amazon, must 'leverage gift cards for ... rewards'.[32] This is a highly racialized system: the platform offers most European countries the option of bank transfers, while workers in counties from the Global South – such as Botswana, Qatar and South Africa – only receive gift card points. In these countries, the platform comes to resemble a kind of digital company town, where tasks are completed for tokens only spendable on services and goods provided by Amazon. Even those lucky enough to receive cash for their labour may, ultimately, have little access to it. Before changes were made to Mechanical Turk's payment system in 2019, many Indian workers were paid via cheques. These were often lost en route, or were else not cashable – not least because slums and remote villages often have limited postal services and no access to banking facilities.[33]

The wages of microwork are nearly always less than the universal contractual form so often invoked by capital's fabulists and boosters. They certainly do not add up to the $40,000 figure plucked as if from thin air by the World Bank. This is a significant but unremarked feature of platform capitalism: the workers turning masses of data into the valuable information that sustains the system are waged only in the loosest sense. Microwork sites allow large platforms to hide this reality or at least to make it seem acceptable. The workforces of Google and Microsoft exist behind a marketing mirage that sustains a sense of microwork as not quite work, the microworker not quite a worker. Far too often, the requesters receive all of the work without having to pay a worker. Only for those actually doing the work does the sentiment ring hollow: getting paid to not do much really means doing a lot to not get paid.

Humans-as-a-Service

Like others who somehow manage to subsist on informal service niches, microworkers have no obvious occupation. 'Microworker', 'crowdworker' and 'humans-in-the-loop' are just some of the nebulous terms that try to reimagine this negative space as something coherent. There is, of course, the initial problem that the term 'microwork' originates with Samasource, a platform to which refugees represent little more than grist for the AI mill. The term tacitly serves the interests of such actors, who, along with institutions like the World Bank, wish to dignify an essentially immiserating pursuit. Indeed, there is a tendency to use 'microworker' as if the term described a proper profession with routine and specific tasks, like 'lawyer' or 'doctor'. But microwork is, by its very nature, highly contingent, irregular and essentially formless. Jeff Bezos perhaps best describes this void – albeit unintentionally – in his shameless marketing of Mechanical Turk as 'humans-as-a-service'.[34] Though evoking 'software as a service' in an effort to disguise labour as computation, Bezos also captures the vacuity of a role that ranges over a multitude of tasks, often cleaved from other jobs. All of this leaves us with a question: what precisely is microwork if not an occupation?

The decline of the occupation began at the turn of the nineteenth century, when the division of labour and its associated roles underwent a sweeping transformation. The birth of the capitalist system changed the nature of production and, in so doing, the nature of work itself. What was once the product of a single worker became a social product, the result of many hands and minds working in cooperation, a division of labour that continues to become ever more divided.[35] Over the course of the twentieth century, this process followed the path of capital into the service sector, with financial and legal services as well as hospitality and retail now employing a highly stratified workforce. Unlike a smaller independent store, where an owner may perform all the tasks required to keep it ticking over, a large supermarket splits the labour among shelf stackers, checkout clerks, stock checkers, customer service, deli workers and managers. While some occupations all but vanish during waves of automation, others materialise, not least because of the need to invent new, niche services to keep a growing redundant mass in work – again, think of online dating assistants, pet therapists and various stripes of 'consultant'.

Yet as occupations – and perhaps pseudo-occupations – flourish in quantity, they tend to wither in quality. Occupations, in a more perfect form than our current labour market now allows for, once entailed inherited skills, knowledge and cultures, personally passed down over generations. This, the essence of true occupation, Gorz writes, has been in decline for centuries: 'The knowhow of master craftworkers was a *personal* capacity developed during a lifetime in a trade. The craft was something that each craftworker kept improving: learning and progress never came to an end, new skills were acquired and tools perfected.'[36]

Gorz's words of course speak to a world before large-scale industry, when the know-how of a given trade was the sole preserve of the craftworker. Now, complex divisions of labour and advanced technological systems mean most work is no longer personal but impersonal. Know-how ceases to exist in any given occupation, instead residing in the machines that dictate worker activities, the detailed descriptions of tasks created by management and worker reviews gathered from office or factory surveillance. In this sense, the capitalist system not only alienates memory, knowledge and tradition, but experience itself.

Yet, even as technocratic know-how has come to dominate the work process, the spectre of something like Gorz's 'occupation' persists. Automation and rationalization may have made the notion of 'personal' work seem a derisory proposition, but most workers do continue to have a *role* and one that remains consistent day to day, no matter how withered and impersonal it may be. We can think of this consistency as the ghostly outline of what was once called occupation, essentially killed off by machinery and management but still there in some ephemeral sense.

On microwork sites, even these faint traces disappear. Short tasks beamed into phones and laptops no longer add up to an occupation, in any real sense of the word, but to radically fractured, highly transient pieces of other jobs, often lasting thirty seconds or less and bearing little relation to the tasks completed before or after.

This is a particular problem on crude crowd sites, which, unlike their curated counterparts, do not offer the kinds of task packages that provide work for several hours or days. Over the course of a day, a worker on Mechanical Turk might translate a passage from a text; transcribe audio of British accents; show an algorithm how to identify bicycles; write product descriptions for e-commerce sites; flag offensive content; complete a survey about coronavirus; and then visit a McDonalds to photograph 'Happy Meals' and post the pictures online. All the while, the firms who use such sites gain a form of flexibility so absolute they can, in theory, hire and dissolve an entire workforce in the space of a single hour.

Building this degree of flexibility first involves the carving up of existing jobs and projects into short tasks. Take the role of translator. In theory, a great deal of basic translation work can now be done by deep learning algorithms, though many tasks, like translating poetry or fiction, require forms of cultural sensitivity that are not yet programmable. For projects requiring less nuance, a platform like Lionsbridge can help break down larger texts into sections for algorithms and shorter passages workers complete as small tasks. These might include: 'categorization of topics in a conversation, determination of emotions behind a statement, classification of intents and identification of parts of speech'.[37] Rather than hire a few skilled, full-time translators or speech professionals, with rights, a proper wage and access to a union, companies are able to rent a transient team of fifty anonymous workers to fulfil the same role.

To take another example: the much feared (or revered) automation of management is really the decomposition of a unified job into a variety of tasks – some done by machines, others by workers. A common criticism of Uber, for instance, is that the company has entirely replaced managers with algorithms. In reality, much of the managerial role is now split between algorithms and a crowd of workers on platforms like Appen. Consequently, management starts to resemble something entirely unfamiliar. The manager of a taxi company would usually have to supervise a team of drivers, making sure, among other things, that they are safe to be on the road and are who they say they are. Uber has famously struggled with this problem, not least because the facial recognition software it employs is prone to errors. A driver might be flagged as dangerous because their daily photo authentication fails to match their ID on record, perhaps because they shaved their beard or had a new haircut.[38] Because the algorithm is unable to assess the driver's credibility, Uber automatically sends a validation task to a platform like Appen.[39] The worker who accepts the task gets thirty seconds to validate whether the driver is who they say they are. If the worker decides 'yes', the ride goes ahead; if 'no', the ride is cancelled and the driver locked out of their account. For less than a minute, the worker indirectly takes the role of Uber's manager, in effect supervising the algorithm that supervises the labour process and makes decisions about the company's workflow.

Working for twenty different companies over the course of a day, spread across potentially hundreds of disparate tasks over the course of a week, from speech translation to temporarily managing a taxi service, the worker no longer assumes a distinct role but is diversified to the point of occupational negation. One finds a further nail in the coffin of work as a way of life, here described by the historian Perry Anderson:

The bourgeoisie as Baudelaire or Marx, Ibsen or Rimbaud, Grosz or Brecht – or even Sartre or O'Hara – knew it, is a thing of the past. In place of that solid amphitheatre is an aquarium of floating evanescent forms – the projectors and managers, auditors and janitors, administrators and speculators of contemporary capital: functions of a monetary universe that knows no social fixities or stable identities.[40]

As industrialism melted down the solid of bourgeois life into the fluid of modern professions, so now with the growth of artificial intelligence those very professions dissipate into a cloud of tasks, bereft of any trace of culture offered by the relatively fixed occupations of old. This hyperdivision of occupation and income is not limited to microwork. Clickworker and Mechanical Turk are perhaps exemplary of a wider drift toward an economy of service niches, rapidly becoming the standard order of work the world over. A new social polarization beckons – and is perhaps already here – between those with a single stable career and those forced to walk dogs in the morning, clean houses in the afternoon and act as a hired friend in the evening, before searching for online tasks at night.

One of course might wonder whether the end of the colourless simulacra that still passes for occupations would be reason to mourn. Yet, its dissolution into a flicker of transitory moments would simultaneously dissolve the political vectors of the formal labour movement. Already, institutions that once offered a counterbalance to the inexhaustible clout of capital have struggled to adapt to a low-growth economy, where service work – often temporary and precarious – now accounts for over 50 per cent of global employment.[41] Indeed, it's become something of a hoary truism to regard today's petrified union culture as unequipped to organise workers with no fixed occupational identity. Nonetheless, it should be emphasised that those forced to float from petty task to petty task have again been entirely cut adrift by the institutions supposed to support them. Workers on sites such as Clickworker have, to put it bluntly, been left to fend for themselves. At the time of writing, only one union, IGG Metall, has attempted to organise them.

With other kinds of platform labour, something like a stable occupation has proved essential to gaining union access. New unions aimed at organising precarious workers, such as the Independent Workers of Great Britain in the UK, organise couriers and taxi drivers for companies like Deliveroo and Uber. In much of the US and Europe, the regulatory framework for the labour market still privileges the long-term and routine work that comes with occupational status, a regressive throwback to a brief period when so-called 'standard employment' was, for some regions at least, the norm. The continued growth of microwork across Europe and the US threatens to leave increasing numbers of workers without the associated securities of an occupation. Indeed, a recalcitrant underdemand for labour in other areas of the economy will likely mean ever more people in these regions treat microwork as full-time employment, as so many already do in the Global South. To indulge a speculation: as microwork grows in popularity, it may break free from petty data work and incorporate all manner of occupations. Though much work is more efficiently carried out as longer projects and jobs, there is no reason why more white-collar work – such as bits of accountancy, finance, copy, translation and so on – could not be carved up into petty tasks, particularly as these roles are automated ever more heavily. Such a scenario threatens to transform increasing numbers of professionals into wage hunter gatherers.

Microwork, then, hardly represents a new source of 'job creation', as suggested by boosterish reports and articles by the World Bank – 'from millions of tasks to thousands of jobs', promises one such piece.[42] In fact, such articles conveniently invert the logic of a system that aims to convert thousands of jobs into millions of tasks; tasks, no less, that do not readily return jobs. In contrast to the magical thinking of neoliberal optimists, microwork turns on the same illusion as the informal sector, which, Mike Davis concludes, 'generates jobs not by elaborating new divisions of labour, but by fragmenting existing work, and thus subdividing incomes'.[43] The worker patches together a subsistence out of various bits of low-skill labour, prised from the carcasses of other jobs. If something like an occupation can be said to emerge from these economic offcuts then it is surely a Frankenstein monster, the World Bank its gothic alchemist.

In no way a sign of a healthy labour market, then, microwork's prevalence the globe over is a distressing symptom of crisis, where petty tasks are dressed up as proper employment to disguise the catastrophic surpluses that dwarf decent work. Like regimes of accumulation past, platform capitalism moves around the globe searching for the wretched, the damned or those yet to receive the mercy of the market. Only now, with the benefit of information and communication technologies and machine learning, it can source those with truly nowhere else to go – the bare life of a planet in ceaseless turmoil. Unlike previous regimes, it has not forged a new range of occupations for its workforce but effectively maintains a permanent reserve army of market fugitives, only called upon when a piece of work is available.

4

Grave Work

A drone hovers hornet-like above São Paulo's colossal favela Paraisópolis. It traverses the slum's territory, listlessly gliding above the shanties, perhaps to transmit images to the Military Police Operations Centre, a violent state apparatus that mercilessly represses the slum's inhabitants. The drone then drifts over the home of someone who has just logged onto the site Scale, which sources workers across the Middle East and Latin America to label images used to guide automated drones systems.[1] The worker remains unaware of what is taking place above them, just as they remain unaware of the purpose of their work. Whether the tasks power autonomous weapons systems raining disaster down on slum districts or else power geographic data for humanitarian agencies that provide aid to such disaster zones is knowledge not available to the workers. Nothing about the tasks in and of themselves reveals their purpose. Workers remain at the behest of the good faith of requesters to offer such information – an extravagant kindness one would imagine is rare.

If microwork represents a shift in the contours of informal sector work it also announces a new, dismal instalment in the treatment of those marginal to the wage. In ways beyond Marx's most vivid nightmares, the poor and dispossessed now unwittingly train the very machines built to track their movements and terrorise their communities, or else replace their role in the labour process. Indeed, it should be emphasised that these nascent methods of platform capital may not represent a divergent economic path so much as omens of a coming world in which the primary or secondary role of most work is to feed machine learning systems. Microwork may, then, represent a crisis of work in its fullest etymological sense: that is, a turning point. Thus, the phenomena described in this chapter are perhaps not merely features of microwork, but early experiments in how to organise a whole range of subemployed pursuits amid capitalist decay.

Black Box Labour

If modern economy triumphed under the aegis of a new rationalist mythos – the worker who freely enters the wage as a rational agent – then microwork either reveals the vacuity of a much-treasured fable or else denotes our arrival in a new world. The answer is perhaps both. The boosterish claims of bootstrap doctrinaires and wage fabulists have, of course, always inflated if not entirely distorted the degree of knowledge available to a given economic actor. Even so, microwork does suggest something of platform capitalism's arrival at a new kind of subject, no longer enlightened by knowledge, but plunged into the darkness of data and the opaque worlds it creates. In certain ways, microwork seems a perfect exemplar of what James Bridle terms our 'new dark age', a refraction of the enlightenment, where tools supposed to illuminate our world throw us into new kinds of techno-induced ignorance and, eventually, barbarism.[2]

But the new ignorance has old class roots. Inequities around who sees and who remains blind have undoubtedly been aggravated by recent innovations in 'Big Data', so many of which are perhaps more bluster than reality, with companies like the data analytics consultancy Acxiom confidently promising clients a panoptic '360-degree customer view'. But capital has long claimed the status of prophet, often by simply impeding the vision of workers. The difference now perhaps is that, as algorithms make ever more decisions automatically, ever more of reality takes place behind our backs. For algorithmic sorcery to remain the rarified precinct of data mystics and arbitrageurs, new kinds of economic blindness must be conjured.

Myopia undoubtedly affects those at the furthest reaches of other supply chains too – someone stitching garments in Bangladesh for Primark may not know, ultimately, which company their labour serves. More generally, the factory worker or shop assistant remains unaware, on some level at least, of their exploitation – hence the oft-quoted line from Marx's *Capital*, 'they do not know it but they are doing it'.[3] But workers do know they are producing a tyre for a car or selling a garment for someone to wear. Even someone working for a company that manufactures nuts and bolts for distant military contractors is able, with some research, to figure out the nature of their work. Microwork, however, thins the aperture of knowledge to a tiny sliver of light, divesting workers of the capacity to know what they are doing and to what end. The Bangladeshi tailor knows they are making a shirt for someone to wear, even if they do not know which company will eventually sell it. The shirt has a tangible use the tailor can readily perceive. The worker on Clickworker, on the other hand, often has little idea of what they are creating. One might say that, in every instant the tailor can see, the microworker is blind.

This is in no small part because the tasks exist at such a high degree of abstraction it becomes impossible to relate them to anything like a meaningful whole. More importantly, though, microwork sites are 'like clandestine installations on unmapped territory; too little is known about them'.[4] Unlike the nuts and bolts made by a worker for Ford, the coffee served for Starbucks or the survey handled by a call centre worker, the products of microtasks are often hidden away from workers for reasons of secrecy. When transcoding audio of voices, the worker knows they are putting into writing the words of a speaker with an Irish accent. But there is no sense of what this recording actually is (e.g., data for a chatbot algorithm) or how it will be used (e.g., to automate fast-food restaurants). Such information is concealed by big tech cabals who rely on microwork sites to facilitate projects of a secret nature.

Google's use of microwork for a US Department of Defense initiative, Project Maven, is a case in point.[5] In one of many secret deals between the US military and big tech, the Pentagon contracted Google to develop an artificial intelligence program capable of sorting thousands of hours of drone video, ultimately with the goal of helping the military identify targets on the battlefield. For the program to be useful, it would need to learn how to differentiate objects into 'buildings', 'humans' and 'vehicles'. Partly to keep costs low, but also to keep the project private, Google contracted the services of Figure Eight (now Appen), a microwork site that specialises in data annotation. Via the Figure Eight platform, taskers then provided algorithms with the requisite data sets by identifying objects in CAPTCHA-like images taken from the footage. In so doing, workers unwittingly helped Pentagon officials to engage in 'near-real time analysis' – to 'click on a building and see everything associated with it'.[6] The anonymity here afforded Google, alongside the highly abstract nature of the videos, meant workers could not see who they were working for and what they were working on – a drone video does not immediately reveal itself as a tool of war, likely appearing as innocuous footage of an urban area.[7]

A team of sociologists found that workers annotating data for autonomous vehicles similarly had little idea about what they were working on:

Some respondents mentioned a task they called 'motocross' where they had to identify roads and tracks in photographs and to indicate the nature of the ground (pebbles, road, sand, etc.). Some thought it was for a video game, others for a census of racetracks. This is because, as we soon realized, requesters vary widely in the extent to which they provide detailed information on their tasks, and on the purposes they serve, leaving workers often confused.[8]

This is a particular problem when – as with Project Maven – the technologies supported by microwork are built for explicitly oppressive ends. A particularly grim example: requesters are not obliged to state that face-tagging tasks – common across all platforms – are used to train facial recognition algorithms. Modelled on eugenicist theory, the software is used to capture people's faces and compare the photos to existing databases, with the aim of identifying and locating people – often producing highly racist results.[9] Only the latest strategy in the militarization of urban space, facial recognition has unleashed a police armageddon on poor neighbourhoods, most notably in the vast carceral cities of Los Angeles and Shanghai. The LAPD has used the software around 30,000 times since 2009, often to defend richer enclaves from 'gang crime'.[10] In the wake of Covid-19, use of the software was ramped up across the globe, but most evidently in many Chinese cities. Ostensibly used to help track the virus, the technology's more obvious purpose has been to track and detain minorities. Most disturbingly, the technology has been central to an ethnon-ationalist cleansing project that has seen the Chinese state intern growing numbers of the Uyghur population in con-centration camps. The state-owned 'commerce' platform Alibaba now offers clients software that has the express purpose of identifying Uyghur faces.[11]

The tasks that power these authoritarian nightmares are central to the service platforms like Mechanical Turk offer to requesters.[12] More pertinently, Amazon likely uses the service internally to train its own controversial software, Rekognition, described by the company – in terms as vague as they are sinister – as a tool for monitoring 'people of interest'.[13] That the software has been contracted to many police departments and pitched to a number of security agencies, including US Immigration and Customs Enforcement (ICE), only further suggests its racialized targets.[14] Recent decisions by IBM, Amazon and Microsoft to stop contracting these technologies to police departments seems more a considered calculation of the PR risks in light of growing support for Black Lives Matter than a genuine ethical commitment, suggesting that if or when support wanes such deals will be back on the table.

Other companies such as the menacingly named Clearview AI continue without shame or mercy to contract the software to agencies like ICE.[15] The short data tasks that ultimately benefit these agencies are entirely divorced from the oppression they conjure, lacking descriptions that directly link them to the technology or any indication of which firms are contracting them. Unable to see who or what the tasks empower, workers blindly develop technologies that facilitate urban warfare and cultural genocide. It is a grim irony that the refugees who use microwork sites are effectively forced to create the very technology that directly oppresses them, a further though by no means new twist in the capitalist tale of machines subjugating workers to racist structures.

Part of the problem is the sheer number of sites and interfaces among which workers are shuttled on a daily basis, making identifying the kind of work one is involved in close to impossible. The platform for which work is actually being completed hides behind complex multi-layered structures, whereby different roles are taken by different sites. The worker might believe they are completing tasks on YSense, when in fact the platform is only acting as an agent for Appen, itself hosting tasks for Google.[16] As corrupt avatars for big tech, microwork sites hide the new satanic mills of firms that 'do no evil'.[17]

Vendor management systems (VMSs) add a further layer of opacity to already murky chains of outsourcing.[18] These systems recruit and supply workers for sites like Microsoft UHRS and Google Raterhub, acting as agents that in some cases pose as microwork platforms in their own right. Further obscuring the waters, some companies like Clickworker act as microwork sites and VMSs simultaneously, hosting tasks from a range of smaller requesters as well as supplying labour to bigger clients like Microsoft UHRS. VMSs are often used by larger platforms in tandem with nondisclosure agreements (NDAs) to keep their use of microwork quiet. For instance, Google used a VMS to hide workers on EWOQ, the company's highly enigmatic precursor to Raterhub.[19] Such diligent attempts to vanish its raters are more fundamentally efforts to conceal the secrets that power its predictive PageRank algorithm, utilising the same methods of NDAs and VMSs that Facebook uses to contract moderators and fortify its own algorithmic edifice.

As the world's poor are corralled into helping a platform plutocracy predict the future, the present necessarily becomes a less predictable terrain. Effectively working inside a black box, workers are divested of all the usual ways to orient themselves inside the labour process.[20] There are no managers, only algorithms; no fellow workers, only avatars of competitors; no obvious points of contact or information. Work is a realm of 'unknown unknowns', of shadows playing across the wall and 'black swans' appearing out of the dark, where all that remains visible is the task directly in front of them. Big tech companies lurk in the shadows, tasks are obscure, while accounts are closed and requesters vanish without warning. Blind and isolated, one struggles to see what one's labour precisely is and who it benefits, just as one struggles to defend oneself against an employer about which nothing is known.

The worker, then, plays nightwatchman to a shadowy algorithm. They may know that training data is fed into the algorithm and that a decision comes out of the other side, but what goes on in between remains entirely opaque.[21] This opaque space represents a black box, a dark patch covering something of significant social effectivity, entirely impenetrable – for reasons often of power and secrecy – to those outside its workings. Hidden is how the algorithm makes the decision – on what grounds, for whom and with what aim. As appendages to these algorithms – refining, enhancing and supervising their capacities – workers spend their days in this shadowy netherworld, neither able to see the process on which they labour nor readily seen by those outside its parameters. This is how larger platforms want their labour: obscure to those doing it and invisible to the wider world.

Workers without a Workforce

The aim, however, is to conceal not just a wider labour process, but workers from each other. Platform interfaces provide no messaging services or profiles that workers can access. This is partly to foreclose potential militancy but more fundamentally to prevent a workforce, in any conventional sense, from coming into existence at all. Thousands of workers in contact with each other would heighten the risk of a secret project being made public. But it would also threaten to dispel the algorithmic illusion and thus disrupt the financial interests these sites uphold. The threat is no more palpable than to firms using microwork to disguise their workers as machines in a bid to attract venture capital. As Lilly Irani points out:

By hiding the labour and rendering it manageable through computing code, human computation platforms have generated an industry of start-ups claiming to be the future of data. Hiding the labour is key to how these start-ups are valued by investors, and thus key to the speculative but real winnings of entrepreneurs. Microwork companies attract more generous investment terms when investors perceive them as *technology companies* rather than labour companies.'[22]

For the whole nexus of corporate reputation, financial circuitry and technological spectacle that sustains platforms to remain intact, workers must remain out of sight. Whether for the purposes of sourcing venture capital or concealing a clandestine project, microwork vanishes big tech's dirty little secrets. In place of workers one finds a cheerful pageantry of machines, an exhibition of innovation and fanciful valuations. All that can be seen from the outside is the apparent successes of entrepreneurs and programmers, not the mundane exploitation of day-to-day capitalism. To achieve this, workers must be kept apart, not only by oceans and borders but by software interfaces that segregate the workforce, making it not only invisible to requesters but to itself.

In the wake of the Covid-19 pandemic, the tactics by which this is achieved are increasingly valorised under the rubric of remote work. Work outside of the workplace, taking place either in living rooms or coffee shops, perfectly harmonises with the model of labour Silicon Valley has been incubating over the last decade, one where workers never meet or communicate. This forms a single aspect of the cloistered digital world envisaged by the likes of Amazon and Facebook, where all interactions, whether civil, political or economic, take place on platforms accessed from the comfort of our own homes. The postpandemic world is set to be one where the argument for more contact as opposed to less will be an increasingly difficult one to make.[23] Realising this world in the labour market, microwork represents the apex of neoliberal fantasy: a capitalism without unions, worker culture and institutions – indeed, one without a worker capable of troubling capital at all. As if bringing to life capitalism's fever dreams, microwork undermines not only the wage contract, distinct occupations and worker knowledge, but the workforce as unified, antagonistic mass.

Data Nightmares

That the world's jobless and marginalized are being corralled into powering the drones that hover over their homes and the cameras that identify and deport them is perhaps only as depressing as it is unsurprising. There is, however, another more sinister experiment taking place on informal workers in the recesses of silicon capital, of which Mechanical Turk is perhaps exemplary. At first glance, it's not entirely obvious what Amazon gets out of the platform. The site hardly represents a significant venture, at least not in the sense of obvious profits. The sum total that the platform takes from transactions per annum represents, by any calculation, a mere drop in the vast ocean of Amazon's annual revenue. Factor in the costs of running the site and its profitability seems somewhat dubious.

But reading through the small print of the site's terms and conditions for workers, it soon becomes obvious what Amazon's real agenda is: 'The Task content that you upload and work product that you receive via the Site may be retained and used to improve the Site and other machine learning related products and services offered by us'.[24] Given more than a second's glance, one realises these words suggest something rather novel: each task

72

completed on the platform automatically sends Amazon a precise data set about how it was completed. Mechanical Turk may appear as a labour broker, an intermediary that takes a cut for hosting exchanges between workers and employers, but its real purpose is to provide data for Amazon Web Services.[25]

Just as Mechanical Turk allows Amazon to broaden the scale and scope of its data capacities, many smaller microwork sites have data-trading agreements that benefit larger platforms. In its online terms and conditions, Playment states that 'the work-product the User collected and/or generated whether by answering questions, taking photos etc. becomes Playment's property.'[26] Because the product described here is labelled or categorised data – a nonrivalrous resource – both requester and Playment can enjoy its use simultaneously. Like Mechanical Turk, Playment receives the data content of a task simply by acting as an intermediary. But unlike Mechanical Turk, which operates solely for Amazon's interest, Playment shares this data with third parties, one of which is Facebook.[27] The social media site is used by Playment to build up profiles of its workers' friends and predict which of these contacts might also want to work on the site. In the process, we should expect that Facebook receives a wealth of annotated data on a variety of tasks.

While the privacy terms and conditions for other sites are not available unless one signs up for work, one can speculate with some certainty that Raterhub grants Google access to Appen's vast trove of labour data and that Microsoft uses UHRS to access data on Clickworker. We should think here in terms of data promiscuity, whereby the range of its uses stretches far beyond a company like Microsoft's immediate requirements. A microwork site's ability to attract a client as big as Microsoft or Facebook relies on a perceived ability to grow its and, in the process, the client's access to ever richer and more varied sources of data. Data has a centripetal force in networks, forever moving toward the larger platforms at the centre. To put it another way: because networks are only ever hierarchies in disguise, the more microwork sites a company like Microsoft has in its orbit the greater the range of data it can capture.

It is not entirely coincidental, then, that the financial mechanisms that sustain microwork sites encourage data practises that ultimately benefit larger platforms. To remain solvent, a site like Playment is compelled to collect data to attract capital and grow financial valuations, at least to the extent that venture capitalists regard data-rich platforms as more competitive, efficient and innovative than those without such capacities.[28] In other words, Playment's financial viability rests less on the labour service it provides and more on the data it collects – data which ultimately funnels up to Facebook and Google.

From the platform's perspective – and indeed that of many larger requesters – the utility of the worker may be far closer to a user of Facebook or Google than a wage labourer. The product of the task itself is often less useful than the data about how it was created. One might argue that this simply extends more traditional management strategies of collecting data to optimise organisation and workflow.[29] Because workers on Mechanical Turk contribute data about the work process itself – the ways workers behave, how they complete tasks, when and how often they log in, and how quickly tasks are completed – the data can be fed back into the platform or even into algorithms used in, say, Amazon warehouses, which require a range of behavioural data to effectively monitor and control worker performance.

The surveillance potential finds its bleakest realisation in Chinese data factories, which operate an alternative model of data labelling to remote microwork. Aside from a few large urban plants that, like melancholic testaments to a less automated past, are housed in old concrete and tech factories, much of the industry is emerging in small towns and rural areas, providing work to jobless blue-collar workers, who would otherwise migrate to cities and likely join the country's seemingly boundless informal population.[30] Already numbering over six thousand countrywide and taking over the employment of entire villages, these airless 'data farms' are likely to stretch as the century progresses into digital company towns or even data haciendas, where whole rural expanses are converted into tech-owned estates to which a dispossessed migrant class is effectively shackled.[31] Unlike their remote counterparts on Appen and Lionsbridge, workers are penned up in offices that in their bland claustrophobia bear more than a passing resemblance to call centres. The close proximity of workers makes it easier for companies to collect physiological data than from those working remotely. As the worker completes a particular task, say, labelling medical images, the company records their gaze and bodily movements such as keyboard strokes, the time they take to complete the task, and how accurately they do so. Management becomes an unbearable kind of scrutiny, a continuous surveillance of the worker's bodily responses in high definition. By mapping the labour process so intricately, managers can steer specific tasks to high-performing workers in real-time.[32] By the same token, given their precarious status, low-performing workers can be readily discarded by hawkish algorithms.

The 'algocratic' oppression of today's digital Taylorism differs only in extent from the management styles of twentieth-century economy.[33] The real difference lies outside of management, in the use of data to enhance machine learning services. Hovering over every exchange between requester and worker, Mechanical Turk can, for instance, funnel data from a short translation task into Amazon Translate, an automated neural network machine provided by Amazon Web Services (AWS). Amazon gets all of this data simply by acting as host. Here we find the primary function of Mechanical Turk: a barely profitable, potentially even unprofitable, labour platform cross-subsidising Amazon's wider business operations as a logistics and software company.[34] Mechanical Turk is interested less in the levy on transactions, more in the data about the work process.

The worker as engine for machine learning is not such an absurd proposition when considering the idiosyncrasies of a company like Amazon's wider business model. In many respects, much of what Amazon does differs little from the model of Victorian capitalism. Precarious labourers are still marshalled into warehouses and compelled to endure long hours to package goods and churn out surplus capital. But Amazon is less the 'everything store', more a universal logistics system. As Malcolm Harris drolly notes, 'more than a profit-seeking corporation, Amazon is behaving like a planned economy.'[35] The vast warehouses, the delivery vans, the Amazon stores are all physical expressions of a computerized logistical system which distributes labour, goods and information. Every aspect of Amazon's business model is geared toward enhancing its computational power. Amazon Prime, for instance, loses money on each order, and only exists to attract customers onto the platform who leave the data required to power its logistics and cloud services. As Kim Moody notes:

> Information technology links all aspects of logistics from the movement of goods over roads, rail, air, sea, to the various distribution and fulfilment facilities and their internal functioning. Huge data warehouses or centres are a key part of this physical supply chain infrastructure and central to the effort to speed up and smooth out the movement of goods and money.[36]

76

In the process of becoming a logistical giant, the company developed AWS, initially an internal service for data storage, software applications and computational power that has since come to provide the majority of Amazon's operational income.[37] Now the global leader in cloud computing, AWS provides governments with data storage space, the military with algorithmic power and other companies with logistics solutions and machine learning. Ever more businesses and governments now rely on Amazon to organise and store their data, which takes an infrastructure just as large as the one for physical things, comprised of huge data centres expanding in number and size every year.[38]

Like Google's knowledge monopoly and Facebook's 'social industry', Amazon's logistics behemoth displays an increasingly totalitarian style of economy.[39] The growing number of partnerships between the tech giants, as well as their contracts with various government agencies, stage a ghoulish capitalist politburo that aims to deliver a kind of data-determined social harmony, as enchanting as it is ruinous.[40] One can reasonably conclude that in this imagined future, the principal means of expropriation is no longer the wage relation but data capture, where the platform class no longer relies on labour so much as social activity, drawn from the habits and movements of day-to-day life. Looking at the range of services the platform giants hope to one day automate – warehouses, delivery, human resources, health and finance, to name but a few – we see a future in embryo, one in which the wage is effectively abolished, in which huge conglomerates stretching into cosmic totalities continue to own and control the means of production but no longer employ people, whose primary role is simply to feed machines data via their daily activities. This imagined future haunts the world of microwork, where data about a task is often more important than the task itself. Work as a productive activity becomes secondary, but it does not disappear. Rather, in becoming increasingly marginal to the interests of a system no longer creating jobs, it permeates the entire social landscape, as workers desperate for income are forced to turn every waking hour into monetizable activity. A global 'servant economy' beckons, writes Jason E. Smith, which 'would push commercialism into the deep pores of everyday life, and make resisting it a crime. You would have to treat people kissing each other for free the way they treated poachers in the nineteenth century.'[41]

Unwittingly or unwillingly, microworkers are corralled into doing the tasks that promise such a world. No mere speculations, such visions are like refracted images of our own stagnant economy of miserable service work, presided over by an increasingly authoritarian state-market nexus, which in recent years has found a faithful lieutenant in the AI industry. The latter of these qualities puts us in mind of the Chinese state, wherein a repressive repertoire of ubiquitous facial recognition, biometrics and personal device tracking has been enlisted toward a growing social credit system that rewards conformity and punishes subversion.

Silicon Valley, of course, has its own authoritarian impulses. A far-right contingent – computer scientist Curtis Yarvin, blood-drinking cofounder of PayPal Peter Thiel, and proto-fascist politico Steve Bannon – has coalesced around the ideas of the neoreactionary prophet Nick Land. Land's theoretical work, broadly in the accelerationist tradition, triumphantly forecasts a 'runaway process' in which, under the auspices of AI, capital entirely pulls away from human life.[42] In this nightmarish scenario, the whole vista of antagonisms between capital and labour would effectively vanish in the total shadow of capital's dominance. Such ideas furnish a neoreactionary milieu that sees democracy as anathema to the smooth functioning of an automated society and that proposes to replace democratic states with CEO monarchs. As eccentric as they sound, these ideas are not peripheral to the Silicon elite but comprise, in the words of Dyer-Witheford et al., 'part of the cultural ambience of AI.'[43]

Even if we resist the jubilant fatalism of Land's protofascist nightmare, the less extreme scenario in which automation continues to work its way – however slowly – through a stagnant economy will still lead to significant human misery. It is this miserable arcadia that the supposedly more respectable sections of the Silicon elite have in mind. Perversely tasked with building this future are the workers of Appen, Playment and Mechanical Turk. Processing the data and powering the algorithms that make autonomous vehicles and smart cities possible, their implicit role is to erase their own work and that of others. The data they process powers the chatbots replacing fast-food workers, the delivery bots displacing couriers and the lights-out manufacturing set to supplant factory workers. The algorithms they oversee remove the need for supervisors and managers. Google and Facebook have been clear that the ultimate role of content moderators is to automate their own jobs away.[44] In doing so, microworkers fulfil the tragic function of expediting labour's superfluity. Already, 'any question of the absorption of this surplus humanity has been put to rest', Benanav and Clegg grimly note. 'It exists now only to be managed: segregated into prisons, marginalized in ghettos and camps... and annihilated by war.'[45] Now these refugees, prisoners and victims of occupation are forced into microwork by law or circumstance, to undertake the grave work of furthering the superfluity of others. The refugee in Kenya's Dadaab camp, the inmate of a Finnish prison, the jobless Rust Belt worker, all represent the surplus humanity compelled to make more of humanity surplus.

5

Wageless Struggle

Is there any possibility of organising workers, then, who destroy the foundations of their own employment? The answer might better be subsumed within a wider question: do the growing mass of informal workers, day labourers and 'microentrepreneurs' possess the agency to create power on the scale of earlier working-class movements? Riots, wildcat action and violent upheavals are moments in a long and fractured history of surplus struggle. From Marx onward, writers have warned that this struggle at all times threatens to fall under the spell of reactionary impulse.[1] The 'lumpen' must be organised, these writers argue, else a 'politics of inferno' beckons.[2] In the politics of such neofascist sorcerers as Jair Bolsonaro, Nahendra Modi and Donald Trump, the inferno is today raging, as age-old alliances between a downwardly mobile middle class and the dispossessed reassert themselves, and as growing numbers look to reactionary forces for security and hope. But it also burns in the cities set aflame by the riots and revolts that represent an ever more common feature of twenty-first-century life. From the burning of buses and stations in Santiago and the unfurling upheavals of Hong Kong, Ecuador and Iran, to the cindered shadows of police stations in Minneapolis and Los Angeles, a grand spectacle of the futureless has set the night on fire.

These, then, are the stakes: that the wretched and precarious, left disorganised, fall under the thrall of reactionary elements, or else are prone to riot intermittently at the system's edges. That there is no scenario imaginable in which this vast surplus is reincorporated into capital only sets the stakes higher still. As the neoliberal moment reaches its melancholic coda, strategies to resolve surplus humanity tend toward an ominously Malthusian tenor. A death cult consensus has ordained that – to stall the slow apocalypse of slums, war, debt and now the rapid armageddon of climate catastrophe – simply affix 'micro-' to finance, enterprise or work. A grim solutionism betrays only the interests of Silicon Valley and Wall Street billionaires. Empty promises substitute for true motivations to return the wretched to humanity. That microwork sites offer 'jobs' or 'skills' are just two such promises this book has attempted to show as the fictions they are.

One might reasonably speculate that such promises account for why these sites have seen no mass walkouts, no acts of data sabotage or algorithmic disruption, only a crowd so quiescent that accounts of the surplus as atavistic seem entirely misplaced. For this reason, one might wonder whether microwork offers a route to trouble capital at all. It is evident that – taken by sufficient numbers – strike action would ripple across the system as a whole. AI projects would sink as venture capital stagnates; algorithms would make unwanted decisions and dangerous mistakes. Even on a smaller scale, a strike by content moderators would instantly swamp user feeds with violent and pornographic images.

But disruption on this scale is smothered before it can catch light. A message of solidarity from content moderators to Facebook employees, who chose to walk out after the firm failed to stop President Trump from using the site to incite racist violence, encapsulates the risks such workers face:

We would walk out with you – if Facebook would allow it. As outsourced contractors, non-disclosure agreements deter us from speaking openly about what we do and witness for most of our waking hours... In contrast to the official Facebook employees, NDAs also prevent us from voicing concerns and contributing to the public discussion about inevitable ethical challenges connected to the job. We would walk out with you – if we could afford it. At the moment, content moderators have no possibility, no network or platform or financial security – especially when we are atomized in pandemic and remotely micromanaged – to stage an effective walkout without risking fines, our income and even our right to stay in the countries where we live and work.[3]

Paralysed by legal and software architectures that replace bodies with avatars, crush conflict with account closures, or else gag users with NDAs, workers stand at a growing pressure point unable to make a move. The more general that AI becomes to producing and circulating bodies and things, the more fragile capital is to disruptions affecting the flow of data. But the more machine learning suffuses the labour process, smoothing tensions through surveillance and gamification, the less likely disruptions become. As algorithmic control suffocates worker action before it can take a breath, too readily is the shout of the crowd sublimated into the gentle hum of software code.

Such inertia is not unique to microworkers but displays the wider torpor of today's worker movement, unable to move against a system no longer reliant on labour to anything like the degree of the postwar period. In the twilight of industrial growth, bargaining power has diminished, union membership has declined and, as the aborted democratic efforts of Bernie Sanders and Jeremy Corbyn suggest, conditions necessary for something like a mass labour party – dependent as it is on a now largely defanged worker movement – have all but vanished. Platforms have moved into the space evacuated by worker power and have reasserted capital's dominance over labour in ways reminiscent of the early industrial period. It is hard not to conclude that this 'late-capitalist triage of humanity' has foreclosed all avenues for labour.[4]

Unities without Unions

Defined by superfluity, exclusion and informality rather than a wage, microworkers pose a particular challenge to labour organisers, whether looser worker associations or the more typical institutions of organised labour. Everything from the international geography of microwork to the pools of surplus labour on which platforms draw makes their organisation an uphill struggle. Monthly or annual models of union membership run up against microwork's temporal dynamics, with workers joining sites daily and some staying for only brief periods. With 'contracts' between microworkers and requesters lasting mere minutes, sometimes only seconds, wages are so volatile that membership fees are likely unaffordable.

Even if unionization were financially viable, unions so often relate to their members through identities of a professional or occupational nature, to which microwork offers only an unequivocal negation. One finds no clearly demarcated occupations, no sectors or vocations, only the loose array of odd jobs so typical of our low-growth economy. New unions like the Independent Workers of Great Britain (IWGB), which organises workers by precarious contract rather than occupational status, offer rays of light against this bleak backdrop. But even if such unions were the rule rather than the exception, microwork often takes place in slums, camps, prisons and occupied territories, places where unions fail to reach and organising ranges from dangerous to criminal activity.

84

Even outside of these more extreme spaces, workers tucked away in bedrooms and internet cafes remain invisible to one another and to the institutions that might otherwise organise them. Workers are geographically dispersed, rarely if ever brought together in physical space. On labour platforms where action has been effective, meeting in town and city centres has been a central tenet of organisation. As Callum Cant, a key organiser on Deliveroo, explains:

> Deliveroo began to further increase the labour supply... More riders started working every evening, but the number of orders stayed the same. That meant that we worked less, earned less and spent more time at the zone centre. As we stopped going drop to drop, everyone started to get to know each other. I got used to starting work by joining a crowd of between five and thirty workers waiting at the cyclists zone centre.[5]

Attempts to discipline workers by flooding supply only served to bring together an otherwise fragmented workforce and provide the grounds from which to organise. Such face-to-face meetings seeded a swell of wildcat strikes in Brighton, London, Southampton, Newcastle, Oxford, and other British cities.[6] Yet, this chain of events is hard to imagine being set in motion by those who encounter each other only as online avatars. Organisation thrives on a public dimension that microwork sites prevent, not only by geographical distance but software frontiers that limit worker contact.

Such barriers restrict organisation to the less than ideal terrain of online forums. Users of TurkerNation and MTurkGrind, as well as Turker-themed Reddit threads, engage in small-scale, nonantagonistic action such as raising funds for fellow workers.[7] Such action has been most effective when aimed at the architectures of specific sites. Pushing back against one-sided review systems, Turkers have developed Turkopticon, a website and browser plug-in that overlays the worker's screen and allows them to write reviews about requesters and publish them in real time.[8] The simple fact of the tool's existence – letting requesters know they might be rated – itself acts as a deterrent against wage theft and other misdemeanours. But while the plug-in helps to discipline requester behaviour, it is not built to transform the platforms themselves. Alone it carries little potential as a tool for mass mobilisation, even if it does show that workers can collectively organise. Built to modulate requester behaviour rather than to unleash worker power, its role remains more reform than revolution.

The impact of efforts to make platforms behave better has been as limited as other attempts to tame capital's nastier elements. In a 2011 letter-writing campaign, workers on Mechanical Turk wrote to Jeff Bezos asking him to raise the price of their labour and improve the site's functions. The letters sought to show Bezos – and the rest of the world – 'that Turkers are not only actual human beings, but people who deserve respect, fair treatment and open communication.'[9] In one letter, the CEO was told in no uncertain terms: 'I am a human being, not an algorithm.'[10]

Hosted on We Are Dynamo, a forum set up for and by workers to organise on the site, the campaign remains the only action Turkers have successfully organised. During the forum's limited period of operations members could post campaign ideas and vote on those of others, giving workers a means to mobilise around popular suggestions. It aimed, in the words of its architects, to create 'publics that are just large enough to take action – unities without unions', standing in for more traditional labour institutions that had so far ignored the site or were otherwise unable to represent its users.[11]

But We Are Dynamo did not last long. The site relied on Mechanical Turk to host tasks verifying the status of new members as real 'Turkers'. Once Amazon realised what was happening, it immediately closed Dynamo's account, cutting off the forum's source of new members.[12] That We Are Dynamo was so quickly defeated indicates the Sisyphean task such workers face as they attempt to organise collectively.

The letter campaign still represents the sole action taken by Turkers. And though effective at drawing media attention to those working on the platform – arguably a first step toward more robust forms of action – the campaign's result was to humanise rather than organise workers. The limits of such action mirror the limits of an atomized workforce, forced to meet through informal online means, and unable for lack of power or money to turn action into something more durable. It is perhaps not surprising, then, that no such campaigns have appeared around sites such as Playment and Appen.

To condemn such tools on these grounds, though, would be naive, for at the very least they raise to con-sciousness a common collective struggle. Where the tactics of traditional unions have signally failed to meet the chal-lenges of a digital world, forums and plug-ins have been leveraged into new forms of worker association, even under the menacing shadow of disabled accounts, bad reviews and NDAs. Whether these associations can trans-late a nascent digital militancy into a proper movement still remains to be seen.

Wageless Struggles

An old question hovers over new yearnings: where to for workers lacking a movement? One answer may be the riot. In our age of stagnant growth and financialized accumulation, Joshua Clover argues, '*riot is the modality through which surplus is lived*'.[13] If for Clover the era of production-centred accumulation, stretching from the nineteenth century to 1973, marked the strike's zenith, the present, dominated by finance and logistics, finds a growing surplus, outside of organisation and ripe for riot.[14] In the years following the 2008 crisis, this volatile mass has catalysed waves of insurgency, from riots in London to civil unrest in Hong Kong and Chile, responding to diminished labour demand and price hikes. These outbreaks are the lived antagonism of Fanon's 'wretched of the earth', the eruption of the disorganised and disenfranchised, its ranks filled by the representatives of wageless life: the migrants, convicts and jobless who – thrown to the social margin – exist only to be managed and oppressed by a merciless state.[15]

Clover's schema that splits strike and riot along historical lines, suggesting that the former is giving way to the latter, offers a tempting insight into why microwork has yielded so little that troubles capital. More superfluous than necessary, more wageless than waged, the refugee, slum dweller or jobless worker spasmodically tasked with training Google's algorithms finds their force not on the platform but in the uprising of the dispossessed crowd. The microworkers of Kenya's Dadaab, whose access to a wage is volatile at best, would by Clover's lights be prime candidates for the riots that swept the camp in 2011.[16] The struggle to survive on microtasks encountered by Filipino workers would, perhaps, find its articulation in the San Roque riots.[17]

But Clover is wrong to render wageless struggle in terms of monolithic power blocs. For Clover, the riot emerges *as* the historical subject of our moment: 'The riot goes looking for surplus populations and these are its basis for expansion.'[18] But this has the potentially undesirable effect of removing the agency of those deemed surplus by capital. While some may be irresistibly drawn into the riot's orbit, it should be emphasised that there is no monolithic subject or unilateral trend among global surplus populations. Indeed, over the last few decades various factions of the jobless and subemployed have organised to create movements that go far beyond moments of fleeting exuberance. There are good reasons to believe that these struggles provide a rubric for the future actions of those forced to hunt for a wage online.

Unable to impact production directly, many unemployed workers have revitalised the blockade as a key tactic for disrupting the circulation of people and goods. This tactic was popularised by the Argentinian Piquetero movement of unemployed workers in the mid-1990s, which picketed major highways around Buenos Aires in an effort to force the government to provide better welfare for the city's poor and jobless.[19] Over the twenty-first century, this tactic has become common among unemployed workers the globe over, from laid-off Russian construction workers blocking routes into cities to gain job relief to the unemployed in Bangladesh's Tangail district, who during the Covid-19 pandemic obstructed local highways to secure access to food.[20]

Like their jobless counterparts, informal workers have relied on blockades and barricades. On the Indian subcontinent, rickshaw drivers regularly block thoroughfares with bodies and vehicles to demand improved market conditions. Dhaka in 2019 saw drivers shut down large sections of the city to protest bans on rickshaws in areas being primed for one of the city's many speculative regeneration projects. Following severe traffic congestion across the city, the ban was swiftly lifted by local authorities.[21] Such reluctant capitulation is emblematic of a state response that tends to treat informal workers with contempt, even as it acknowledges their power to grind urban circulation to a standstill. Similar concessions have been made across Latin America to the millions of waste pickers, who – amid the ecological malaise of neoliberal decline – scavenge through trash for a living. Now enlisted by many cities in the battle against climate catastrophe, waste pickers only gained recognition in the eyes of the law by organising and implementing tactics such as blockading dumps.[22] Street vendors in LA have used similar tactics in their ceaseless battle against the city authorities to gain even the most rudimentary legal protections.

Outside of the tightly imbricated divisions of labour that characterise, say, the automotive or oil industries, such action tends to remain at the level of reproduction as opposed to production. In her magisterial study of organisation in India's informal sector, Rina Agarwala reveals a workforce that rarely demands direct wage rises but instead the decommodification of goods in the form of welfare, regulations and rights.[23] The nature of informal work – that workers tend to have no employer or contract – has meant that demands are often targeted at the state. Their success has tended to rely on tactics that disrupt urban circulation to such a degree that governments are forced to make concessions. This is true not only of India but other countries too. Brazil's Homeless Workers' Movement (MTST) strategically blocks the circulation of private housing, preventing new speculative developments by occupying derelict land and handing it to those otherwise forced to reside in slum-like conditions. By disrupting the housing market, the movement has come to play a key role in redefining urban policy around the interests of the city's dispossessed. Here, those excluded from the state-market nexus have contested and – to some degree – won their right to the city.

It is perhaps not surprising, then, that such tactics have imprinted themselves on a new wave of struggles emerging in the platform economy. As platforms bring both the logics and participants of the urban informal sector to the core of accumulation, they have generated demands and strategies that, unsurprisingly, reflect those of 'self-employed' hawkers, rickshaw pullers and couriers.

One of the most remarkable of these upheavals occurred in Latin America under the strained conditions of the coronavirus pandemic. In São Paulo in July 2020, five thousand couriers took part in a historic strike that engulfed the metropolis, resulting in one of the largest mobilisations against platform capital to date.[24] The couriers, colloquially known as 'motoboys', shuttle goods on mopeds around a city that relies on their labour but shows only hostility to their presence. Largely drawn from the Afro-Brazilian population of São Paulo's favelas, motoboys face their expendability on a daily basis, not only in wages too low for survival but in the more brutal form of traffic collisions and assaults – a grizzly phenomenon so ubiquitous that white 'ghost bikes' are now hung across the city to commemorate fatalities.[25] So large is São Paulo's informal sector that there are always other motoboys to replace those killed on the road. Like many of those who find work on Mechanical Turk or Playment, their daily work straddles the formal and informal, spanning everything from messenger errands for casual clients to courier jobs for UberEats and iFood.

The strikes spread across South America to Chile, Argentina and Peru as food delivery platforms expanded their labour supply and relegated existent workers to the status of reserve.[26] Spontaneous, unplanned and appearing outside of the formal labour movement, they materialised as increasing numbers of couriers were drawn to their locus by social media or word of mouth. As support arrived from other sections of the city's dispossessed, workers and nonworkers alike blurred into a bloc of the angry and dejected. In São Paulo – the action's urban nucleus – huge convoys of bodies and bikes blockaded bridges and malls to halt the movement of goods, turning what was originally a strike against a few firms into a city-wide shutdown.

Mirroring the strategies of informal workers across Latin America and the Indian subcontinent, the couriers blocked circulation to immobilise economic activity across entire cities, to press governments to regulate the platforms on which they work. Other platform strikes have focussed even more directly on pushing the state to regulate the economy. To cite only a few examples, strikes by Uber drivers in Cape Town in 2018 and Mumbai in 2019 centred around the demand for lower petrol prices.[27] As workers have been made to purchase the key means of labour – Uber drivers must supply their own vehicles and petrol – their demands have tended to focus on the price of goods. In Cape Town, Uber drivers have repeatedly obstructed central thoroughfares to advance these demands. Similar tactics have been employed by drivers in Paris, who blocked access to the city's airports, and in London, where drivers obstructed access to Westminster and the offices of Transport for London, protesting climate policy that endangered driver livelihoods.[28]

Similar gripes and demands may yet spur microworkers to action. Like Uber drivers and informal couriers, the pains of circulation are felt ever more acutely in the experience of work; microworkers pay for their own laptops, phones, internet access and electricity. And if such pains become unbearable – such as significant price hikes on electricity or poor internet access – then microworkers may band together to take to the streets in protest.

Resistance might, of course, take the form of a digital blockade that impedes the circulation of data. This perhaps only begs the question: in the wispy aether of digital capital, what precisely would a blockade look like? Even if large numbers of data labellers downed their keyboards and mouse pads, a large pool of workers would likely still remain, ready to take the work of those on strike. Labour pools are not geographically limited – like on other sites such as Uber and Deliveroo – but traverse every country where a given site operates, often numbering millions of workers and continually claiming new ones. Anything less than action supported by a great majority of this pool would leave vast troves of tasks to be enjoyed by a refractory few.

As with action taken by other sections of the informal proletariat, microworkers will need to find ways of disrupting circulation that go beyond the mere removal of bodies. Targeted sabotaging of tasks may thus prove a necessary tactic. Its forms might range over mass idling of tasks, to sustained and widespread 'machine breaking', a timeworn tactic that tends to tip into quasi-insurrectionary organisation. The Luddites, British textile militants of the nineteenth century, were one such group which 'continually trembled on the edge of ulterior revolutionary objectives'.[29] In the digital realm, such 'machine breaking' may in fact be little more than a metaphor, so different would data vandalism look to Victorian loom-smashing. Mass derailing of data tasks would be more like a blockade, temporarily stopping data traffic as opposed to actually destroying it – data, unlike a loom, is nonrivalrous, ubiquitous and endlessly reproducible. Nonetheless, there remains an anarchic allure to such action in a moment of algorithmic order. But like other kinds of online action, it would rely on a sufficiently large number of participants so that no one worker could be penalized. Unlike the Luddites, who were masked, disguised and smashed machines under cover of darkness, 'smashing' algorithms would enjoy no such expeditious conditions.[30] Monitored closely, workers fall under the watchful eye of platforms that can shut down action on the spot.

A Wageless Movement?

There is no immediate salvation for a workforce that – like other segments of the precarious and wageless – remains hamstrung by dispensability and fragmentation.

For the waste picker blockading city dumps, the Moto-boys struggling to maintain momentum and for the microworkers whose movement has not yet begun, the best chance of resistance lies in forging wider alliances. Now the destiny of so much of the globe, wageless sur-vivalism poses a problem of acute importance: whether those marginal to the wage can forge a movement as pow-erful as those of the industrial working class. To no less a degree, the future of socialist struggle remains doubtful unless a great section of this mass can imagine new strate-gic levers, points of unification and networks of solidarity. Such an alliance would straddle an economic puzzle of multiple geographies, cultures and identities, and for this reason is, some may argue, fated to failure. Yet strate-gies and demands advanced by organisations such as the Homeless Workers and the Piquetero movement offer workers, unemployed and activists alike the blueprints for a far wider wageless movement. Indeed, if there is to be a coherent antagonism to capital in the twenty-first century, it seems increasingly likely that as ever more become hostage to precarity and redundancy it will be spearheaded by the wageless as opposed to the waged.

Such alliances are anything but inevitable. Graduates in the North's urban centres may work the same tasks as those pushed into slums, penned up in ghettoes or aban-doned to forsaken rust belts. But their relative life chances are still split along national and racial lines, and are only set to widen in a moment of growing crisis. At one end of the spectrum are what the journalist Paul Mason calls 'networked individuals', a mercurial, underemployed, cosmopolitan faction of service workers; and at the other end, a redundant mass, marked out for state repression.[31] International competition for better paid tasks and the contestability of wage prices across national borders can mean the experience of work is often anything but shared. In this way, platforms express a sluggish but hypercompetitive system under which festering precarity only seems to breed resentment, increasingly channelled by reactionary forces into attacks on vulnerable sections of the workforce – women, immigrants and minorities – who offer easy scapegoats for the failures of capital.

But precisely to prevent the dispossessed again becoming the 'bribed tools of reactionary intrigue', greater coalitions of the wageless must emerge, stretching from the underemployed service worker of Berlin to the petit proletariat of São Paulo's favelas.[32]

How, then, might we salvage the forgotten horizon of a workers' international, now in the form of a wageless – not working – class, bound together in common struggle against a system threatening total immiseration and planetary collapse? Such a movement may seem a distant horizon. But many of the minor coalitions, institutions and demands necessary to get there have been gifted already by history.

I. Wageless Associations

Periods of sharply rising joblessness tend to generate movements with the explicit aim of organising the unemployed. After World War 1, amid high levels of out-of-work poverty, most major cities in the UK saw rising numbers of the jobless occupy buildings, blockade streets and stage aggressive confrontations with local authorities. Upheavals initially mirrored the riots we are seeing today, but were later channelled by the UK Communist Party into a wider, more enduring organisation, the National Unemployed Worker's Movement (NUWM).[33] Under the auspices of the NUWM, intermittent outbreaks of conflict cohered into a nationwide hunger march in 1922. Subsequently, the movement saw its membership rapidly climb to around a hundred thousand. Membership fluctuated as the UK economy lurched in and out of crisis, rising precipitously as the unemployed expanded during the great depression. But by 1937 the movement was effectively moribund, as unemployed numbers again began to decline.

In ways that could be emulated today, the NUWM streamlined volatile upheaval into sustained antagonism. Taking many forms, action often sought to bolster that taken by other sections of the dispossessed. Successfully mobilising communities in Sheffield and Glasgow against rising homelessness, the movement helped to stop bailiff evictions, and would regularly frustrate slum landlords by transplanting the furniture of an evicted family into unoccupied accommodation.[34] The NUWM also joined forces with a range of labour unions to help strengthen strikes and settle disputes. Its coherent political position helped to quell the more reactionary elements of the lumpen, namely through antifascist education and action, with pamphlets distributed among its members such as 'Fascist Danger and the Unemployed'.[35]

Though materialising in the 'lost world' of the British communist party, and reliant on a certain amount of militant vanguardism to claim members and organise action, the movements' leaders still tended to rise from the ranks of the unemployed, often skilled engineers who had already cut their teeth at union organising.[36] Though a similar movement must now be made a priority, it must take a different form. Movements built solely around the identity of the 'unemployed' are hostage to the fortunes of a single demographic. Their fates tied to capricious labour markets, they tend to dissolve as the numbers of unemployed drop, their demand for 'jobs' and 'security' met – in however withered a form – as the economy uncoils and expands into new markets. In our moment of slow growth and jobless recoveries, peaks in unemployment after crises tend to disperse the jobless across the growing forms of subemployment, leading to a permanent rise in informal, low-wage work. That is to say, unemployment does not really disappear but simply takes the many guises of precarity, underemployment and in-work-poverty. Somewhat problematically, unemployment and subemployment tend to be treated thereafter as distinct political problems, as opposed to parallel expressions of decreasing demand. Thus, there is a need to organise a movement around an identity more capacious than 'unemployment', to unite all of those expelled from the wage.

Hints of such an identity can be found in Brazil's Homeless Workers' Movement (MTST). As noted earlier, the movement seeks to unite 'workers, laborers, informal, underemployed and unemployed' alike around a common struggle for better housing.[37] Though ostensibly set up to secure formal accommodation for its members, the MTST has mobilised sections of São Paulo's poor against state and capital on a number of political fronts.[38] The demand for decent housing has provided an anchor around which the dispossessed can cohere, a point of common struggle that, one can only speculate, appeals to the survival instincts of motoboy and microworker alike.

II. Wageless Centres

For wider alliances to emerge, those banished from the wage require means to meet in physical space, outside of the strike or protest. Worker centres may offer one strategy for forging face-to-face contact between otherwise disparate sections of the precarious and dispossessed. Adopted as a tactic by migrant day labourers across the US, worker centres offer spaces of communion – 'unities without unions' – for those summoned as cheap labour from abroad then pushed to the nation's fringe. Paul Apostolidis writes at length in his book *The Fight for Time* about their status as spaces of noncapitalist sociality, bringing 'convivial sustenance and mutualist assistance' to those otherwise divided by competition and volatile shift patterns.[39] Over two hundred such centres now exist across the US alone, ranging in their aims from points of advice to spaces to plot against employers. As informal as the workers they cater to, worker centres are not as ideologically restricted as government agencies nor as bound to certain segments of the workforce as unions. For this reason, they can – and often do – offer political education to their patrons.

The potential for centres to establish common bonds across informal workers extends far beyond day labourers and could easily be developed for motoboys, tissue sellers and online taskers. So often these sections of the proletariat exist in a market-driven solipsism, unaware of others facing similar survival struggles. In regions with a high concentration of microwork, for instance, such as the Indian states of Delhi, Karnataka and Maharashtra, centres promise to offer more meaningful and enduring forms of contact than the lonely enclaves of online forums.[40] Physical, brick-and-mortar centres across the world, where people can meet face to face, connected by online spaces that put different centres in contact, would help to cultivate the kinds of communion necessary for a wider movement.

In addition to offering a political education, these centres might reach a more radical position by offering to those long neglected by capital mutual aid and support. Centres could provide food, services and shelter, a scenario where that most fabled of socialist horizons – dual power – again becomes thinkable. Associated with Lenin's definition of the soviets and workers' councils, dual power remains a dormant aspect of today's solidarity networks and mutual aid groups, which, too often bound by the interests of funders or 'service provider' expectations, remain depoliticized. But combined with political tutelage and mobilisation, mutual aid begins to trouble a market whose claim to total jurisdiction over human need and want begins to seem ever more threadbare. When duality is realised to its full extent, 'power moves to the networks to which people turn for practical help and leadership on a daily basis: in effect they become an alternative government, without officially challenging the ostensibly legal structure'.[41]

III. Demands

Many of the recent radical demands that have reinvigorated the political imaginary of the left in the global North have either emerged within or else been taken up by those marginal to the wage. These demands flourished at the peak of the Covid-19 crisis, when capital briefly went into hibernation and left a majority of its participants reliant on state support in one form or another. Sections of the population deemed surplus were forced – either through the threat of death by viral infection or else starvation – to fight for demands that only yesterday were thought to be too radical or else lost to history. These demands have tended to centre around welfare (housing, food, healthcare and education) as opposed to wage increases, and in this regard mirror those of informal workers in countries such as India, who have similarly turned attention away from the wage.[42] Implicitly, many of these demands, in fact, push for a world beyond the wage. Taken together, these efforts invoke a world where life is decommodified on a scale approaching something close to socialism.

Illness and lockdown meant many of the world's most precarious struggled more than ever – and then

refused – to pay energy bills or rent, forcing governments to step in and subsidise payments. The nucleus of
this struggle was the housing market. The pandemic met
a slow-burning crisis of escalating prices, gentrification
and slum dwelling, which as the virus moved through
the global populace erupted into vast numbers unable to
afford their rent. Given the decision between paying their
landlord or starving, large numbers decided to plump for
the latter and pushed for rent amnesties and moratoriums
on evictions. Unprecedented numbers of strikes subsequently swept the UK, the US, South Africa, Brazil, Spain,
Canada, France and Australia.[43]

The impacts of lost income also meant increasing
numbers could no longer afford healthcare, just at the
moment they most needed it. After the Spanish government introduced a second lockdown, protestors in
Madrid called for better, more affordable healthcare pro-
vision. In the east of the country, protestors in Barcelona
carried signs reading: 'More healthcare, fewer soldiers'
and 'Cutting back healthcare kills'.[44] Less fierce but equivalent demands were echoed across Europe and the US.

Privatised food supply chains and distributors were
similarly unequipped to deal with the scale of the crisis.
Lockdowns and fears of catching the virus led to panic
buying that left many supermarkets across the world
looking like the empty shells one sees in disaster films.
Many of those already struggling to afford survival were
forced to rely on mutual aid groups. In the UK, this placed
pressure on the state to provide free essentials to every
household. This prompted further demands for a universal food service, offering every citizen enough food for the
week, as well as access to free delivery and restaurants.[45]

The most radical of these demands grew to deafening
proportions in the wake of the killing of George Floyd,
a black man suffocated by a white police officer, in a
long line of similar deaths. Amid a virus trained on black

life by years of state persecution and economic neglect, Floyd's death proved the final outrage. Straining under the deadweight of black life ended at the hands of white supremacy, history burst into a blaze of protests and uprisings, accompanied by a rousing demand to defund the police. The demand travelled across the Atlantic to Europe and then around the globe, to lives beyond those ritually asphyxiated by capital's agents. It is a demand, however, that carries more than a potential end to police brutality. An institution originally designed to quell the riotous menace that the wretched pose to private property, the police has since developed into a service more directly geared toward economic ends, targeting racialized surpluses as entrants for the prison-industrial complex. Convictions suppress wages as convicts become wageless subjects, forced to labour for petty or no payment as part of their sentence. Once released, they consistently receive lower wages than others, and are far less likely to join unions and strike action.[46] Police and prisons are, thus, an intrinsic part of the US wage system; as Clover pithily notes, 'cops make capital'.[47]

There are, then, in calls to defund the police the traces of a longer history of covert efforts to destroy the wage, not to mention the ongoing campaign for Wages For Housework. To clarify any confusion around the demand, Silvia Federici later adapted its message in a pamphlet titled 'Wages *against* Housework'. The point, as Sophie Lewis provocatively asserts, is not about 'totting up a bill', about gaining a basic income for domestic labour, but 'a process of assault on wage society. It's a noir joke, a provocation, an insurgent orientation', with the ultimate goal of making a utopian horizon possible.[48] In a similarly tacit fashion, calls to defund the police move toward a wageless horizon.

These, then, might represent something like the organic demands of a growing number unable to secure their basic subsistence: free healthcare, utilities, housing and food and an end to unnecessary, violent institutions. Taken together, they reveal a hidden utopian horizon. Some might call it Universal Basic Services (UBS), the idea that services fundamental to human survival should be free at the point of access, and should be democratically determined and managed. But the demands of the dispossessed go further still. They push toward a world where everyone has enough education, healthcare, food and welfare not only to survive but to flourish. Each demand is the refracted image of a world held in common, a vision that opposes our present of abundance for the few and scarcity for the many.

To regard the actions and demands of the dispossessed as a concrete utopia may seem premature. But such an imaginary is now more urgent than at any past historical moment. Capitalism has always been an implausible system, characterised by tensions and antagonisms, ever poised to bring it to the brink of collapse. Today the system's possibility is not only politically but ontologically doubtful, in a way that threatens the existence of life itself. The late capitalist inferno of climate cataclysm and deadly pandemics make the promise of endless growth seem more dubious than ever, even as Silicon Valley conjures wonders approaching the sublime and stock markets spiral toward a bad infinity, bearing little reference to the lives of the many. Even as this increasingly hostile system takes away ever more of what makes life bearable, the majority have learnt to live with it rather than oppose it. Soon, though, our unbearable planet will be an uninhabitable planet. So imagine we must.

Of the many utopian accounts of a world beyond capitalism that have emerged over the last decade, there have been few attempts to seriously reckon with the problem of who brings this world about. As Benanav has wisely warned, 'movements without a vision are blind; but visionaries without a movement are much more severely incapacitated.'[49] Humanity has been told to demand a future.[50] We have been offered visions of what this future may look like, from the techno-utopia of 'fully automated luxury communism' to the ecological harmony of a 'Green New Deal'.[51] Less time, though, has been spent on the question of historical agency and the perennial problem of who will spearhead humanity's transition to a better world. Any renewal of a labour movement resembling that of the twentieth-century now seems impossible. We must look elsewhere.

In the wildcat action and blockades I have described in this chapter, we find the premonitory trembles of a movement emerging. These events suggest the character that political action will take in the coming decades. Whether Covid-19 has truly catalysed a grander vision of where humanity might go remains to be seen. Yet many of the demands that have appeared in its wake offer a common vision around which a larger wageless movement might coalesce. Failing a movement that includes that great number of humanity deemed surplus, there is little room for hope. It is, then, to those long rendered hopeless that hope now turns. For it is to those cast out of the present that the future belongs.

Postscript

A Microwork Utopia?

As the wage goes missing we must imagine what a world might look like beyond it.

Hardly short of futurology, our age of silicon wonders often feels as if our future is being written by second-rate science fiction writers. As an earlier chapter showed, the Dark Enlightenment forebodings of Landian fascism provide a particularly extreme example of the grizzly speculations on offer. Elon Musk's scorched-earth utopia of leaving a dying planet Earth for the red pastures of Mars is not far behind in terms of sheer audacity. Neither of these visions, of course, promises a world without a wage, just a worse form of capitalism, or something that looks like neofeudalism. Like mirages in the desert, they can only lead us to greater despair.

Today's left has also produced its own postcapitalist visionaries, many of whom argue that the technological conditions for a better world are already here.[1] At their best, these visions show us a world of possibility hiding in our seemingly barren present. At their worst, they start to resemble a wish list of technologies. In the aftermath of 2008, these ideas have flourished while our ailing liberal democracies continue to offer debility dressed up as progress.

Comfort can be taken in the fact that today the clearest horizon of a new world can be found in the struggles of the dispossessed. Glimpses of a world with decent housing, education and health care for all flicker at the edges of a dying system. For these flickers to take the form of a true vision, however, will rely on movements such as those described in the previous chapter growing in strength. Such glimpses have appeared cyclically throughout capitalism, when antagonism to the system is at its strongest, in the form of movements and events that can directly challenge the system's hegemony. Today, there is a dreamlike quality to events like the Paris Commune of 1871, where for seventy-two days an insurrection led by the dispossessed turned the city into an autonomous commune. Its spirit was revived in the 1960s commune scene and shimmered across the Occupy movement in the late 2000s. Dreamlike as they may seem, such events are again imaginable in the present moment. For much of the Global North, the experience of capitalism today is perhaps not so different from that of the communards in nineteenth-century France, the majority of whom spent their days hunting for a wage rather than working.[2] What differs, perhaps, is the communard's sheer will of imagination and organisation.

In the struggles that have emerged since 2008, and which were subsequently catalysed during the Covid-19 crisis, the traces of an imaginary similar to that of the commune are again evident – a vision of what Kristin Ross terms 'communal luxury'.[3] Though these traces have not yet taken the form of a real alternative, glimpses of a world where the realm of necessity no longer dominates our lives, where every person has sufficient healthcare, housing, food and education, are peeking into view. These demands provide the lines along which a new world can be imagined, one of social abundance premised on material abundance, where greater freedom and autonomy cover everything from intellectual pursuits to emotional expression.

Many writers have already explored the form that social abundance might take in the twenty-first century. It might mean that all can reach their 'aesthetic capacity', as Ross notes, so that the 'world is no longer divided between those who can and those who cannot afford the luxury of playing with words or images'.[4] Or it might mean a world of relative intellectual and emotional freedom. That is not to argue in some woolly sense for an impossible land of happiness and contentment, but for the possibility of one in which emotions and desires are no longer sublimated to dangerous forms of normativity that generate suffering and subjection. We might assert, as Andrea Long Chu has, that 'the negative passions – grief, self-loathing, shame, regret' deserve to be 'a human right as universal as health care or food'.[5] In light of greater material security, the dominant regime of gender scarcity might be abolished in favour of gender abundance, where 'a hundred sexes bloom'.[6]

Less thought, however, has been given to what the realm of necessity – the labour required to produce such abundance – might look like in a post-scarcity world. The nineteenth-century socialist polymath William Morris argued that such an order must 'attempt to establish society on the basis of the freedom of labour'.[7] This does not mean total freedom *from* labour. Some work would still be necessary to sustain a post-scarcity order. For sure, 'bullshit jobs' would be wholly eradicated, while dangerous toil done by humans for the simple fact that it remains cheaper than when done by machines could be automated.[8] But there would still remain a significant amount of work either beyond the capacity of machines, or else required to forge the social and ecological bonds that sustain human happiness and protect against alienation. As Andre Gorz reminds us, work can offer nourishing forms of community that balance other kinds of communal life, such as the family, which tend toward autarky.[9] For all of these reasons, important debates around what the realm of freedom might look like in a post-scarcity society must be balanced by a clear-sighted vision of what kinds of work will be necessary, and how it will be organised.

The labour required to make sure that everyone has access to food, housing, education and healthcare would be distributed equally across society. Traditionally waged work would be spread equitably, while care and domestic labour would no longer be divided along lines of gender. Women would no longer be forced by violence or coercion to reproduce and spend their lives caring for children and relatives. Indeed, no one would be forced to labour under pains of survival or political duress. 'Necessary' in a society of social abundance would no longer mean 'forced'. Decisions – about who does the work, when, what kind and how much – would be organised democratically. In his classic essay *Useful Work versus Useless Toil*, Morris makes the claim that even the most arduous labour should be made enjoyable. To achieve this, the lines between work, art and play must be blurred wherever possible, the labour itself varied and the working day shortened to no more than a few hours.[10] 'Such a holiday our whole lives might be', Morris concludes, 'if we were resolute to make all our labor reasonable and pleasant.'[11]

Microwork may seem like an odd place to locate Morris's dream of ludic, meaningful work. The monotony of the tasks, the lack of routine, and the insecurity both of income and occupation suggest a kind of work, antithetical to the Eden of Morris's vision. Yet many of these bad qualities are not intrinsic to microwork but the result of a wage relation that robs the work process of satisfaction and meaning. Indeed, the promise that microwork makes to the worker – of an independent, flexible and leisurely working life – looks startlingly similar to the world of work proposed by Morris. In a wage society, this promise is undermined by the fact that these qualities so often denote poverty and precarity. In a wageless society, however, microwork offers a surprisingly attractive vision of how to organise working life, something like a 'concrete utopia' hiding amid our present ruins.[12]

Of particular interest is the sheer range of tasks a worker might undertake over the course of a single day, a degree of variation that thinkers like Morris and Marx understood as essential to work that satisfies individual as well as social need. Microwork operates on principles of flexibility and independence, not because these qualities benefit workers but rather because they allow capital to dodge any responsibility to labour. In a wage society, working for twenty requesters over the course of a day and occupying as many roles in the economy does not, it turns out, offer independence and dynamism, just a dull, relentless struggle for survival. But in a post-scarcity world, where the wage and the associated division of labour have vanished, there is no reason why the small amount of work required could not be as various as the worker's interests.

In its own contorted way, the multifarious tasks undertaken over the course of a single day on a microwork site offers a glimpse of how varied labour might be in a world of communal luxury. As Marx and Engels famously wrote:

> In communist society, where nobody has one exclusive sphere of activity but each can become accomplished in any branch he wishes, society regulates the general production and thus makes it possible for me to do one thing today and another tomorrow, to hunt in the morning, fish in the afternoon, rear cattle in the evening, criticize after dinner, just as I have a mind, without ever becoming hunter, fisherman, herdsman or critic.[13]

Microtasks that disfigure human development offer only a warped version of this vision in hyperexploitative form.

But they push us to question the miserable simulacra of occupations that pass for work under our present system. They demand we rethink the coherence of occupations in a digital age, when jobs can be decomposed into tiny units. Tasks that offer various degrees of damage to the human psyche are, of course, no substitute for the languorous tour of earthly pursuits Marx describes. But if we focus on their organisational form, as opposed to content, it becomes possible to picture the kinds of flexibility writers such as Marx and Morris envisaged. Though the work performed in many roles – such as engineers, medical professionals and teachers – is not divisible to the same extent as data work, the hours necessary for their fulfilment could still be distributed in more equitable and rational ways. Indeed, a wageless society would still require people trained in a particular vocation, but this would neither be their only role nor their primary daily activity, but one of many. One might work as a medic for a few hours one morning and as a farmer the next, and in the afternoons write a novel. There would be enough people trained as medics to make sure that no one person had to perform the role at the expense of a rich and meaningful existence. As Gorz writes:

> Work that is oppressive when carried out all day every day (like sorting the mail, collecting the rubbish, cleaning and repairing) could be no more than a brief interval among so many others if it was distributed among the whole population and therefore took only 15 minutes a day. It could even become a welcome distraction and opportunity for pleasure if, as is already the case with some types of agricultural or forestry work, it were to occupy only a few days a year or a few in a lifetime.[14]

Microwork sites not only evoke a world in which the time of each task is radically reduced, but the time spent working overall. These sites reduce paid labour to a minimum with the result that more of the worker's time is spent hunting for jobs than actually completing them. An archetypal irrationality of a system that makes all dependent on a wage but remains unable to extend a wage to all, this arrangement is not only an inefficient use of labour resources but is also damaging to the worker's body and mind. Under such conditions, fewer hours means less pay and, therefore, a lower chance of survival. But in a society in which survival is no longer conditional on income, and in which all are given the means to thrive, the problem vanishes. Assisted by technology and divested of unnecessary toil, social labour would take up only a slender portion of our days. Much as on microwork sites, machine learning algorithms could be used to calculate and distribute available work, but in ways that privilege free time and autonomy.

Beyond reducing the quantity of work, machine learning could be used to improve the quality of the workers' experience. The feedback infrastructures of big data could be used to distribute work in ways that not only privilege worker performance but also worker preference. Unlike the Chinese data factories mentioned in the previous chapter, where machine learning algorithms decide by past performance which workers get to do which tasks, algorithms could be used to distribute work in a way that prioritises the joys and interests of individual workers.

And finally, gamification need not be a strategy of oppression. Leaving aside the dull economic compulsion that drives the strategies of a managerial elite, we might admit that even today's repressive forms of gamification reference a desire for work to be more playful and enjoyable. In a world without a wage, the promise of ludic labour made by companies such as Playment would be realised as pleasure and play rather than productivity gains. No longer used to impose systems of regulation, rationalization and surveillance on the work process, gamification would be used to make drudgery less monotonous. Machines would not simply be used to save labour costs, push workers harder and reduce the skilled to the toil of the unskilled, but to make work more interesting. Review and score systems might, to some degree, succeed the wage as a means to motivate due effort. Instead of deciding who gets paid and who gets to survive, score systems might act as soft forms of encouragement, playful forms of competition, acting to gamify otherwise gloomy toil. In his 1888 Gilded Age novel *Looking Backward*, Edward Bellamy describes a socialist utopia in the year 2000, where the wage has vanished alongside money, inequality and war. In place of brute economic pressure to work the novel depicts a system of moral and honorific incentives.[15] There is something of these incentives to the public score systems found on microwork sites. But while awards like Mechanical Turk's 'Masters' qualification' offer access to better paid work, in a post-scarcity economy such honorifics might instead be used to impart luminary status, to motivate people to carry out work that is dull or arduous.

The platform economy and the silicon arcadias it promises, then, not only act as a source of regenerative mythology for capital but also a social laboratory in which we may find surprising answers to questions that have long troubled the socialist imaginary. The question of when to use a decision-making algorithm (and when not to) is of little interest to a platform economy in thrall to digital solutionism. Likewise, little thought is given to how flexibility could actually benefit workers, or to how platforms could help provide new motivations for work outside of the wage. These remain questions that any socialist project must confront.

As the previous chapter showed, no project will be successful that fails to incorporate the growing swathes of humanity deemed redundant. But galvanizing a movement able to bring a better world into existence will require a vision of freedom and necessity, a vision that is as credible as it is distinct from a system offering only growing misery and planetary collapse. For most, the present remains tolerable to the extent that the future remains unimaginable. Soon, an unimaginable future may become an uninhabitable future. In response to climate catastrophe, capitalism offers only a techno-solutionism-cum-death-cult. Like sad testaments to the system's nihilism, a facial recognition camera is built to arrest the billions displaced by climate catastrophe, not save them; a chatbot can only jabber its stock phrases as the planet burns.

This failure of imagination is matched only by Silicon Valley's imaginative efforts to exploit the system's casualties, to devise forms of work that offer a life little better than total joblessness. Microwork points to a future where a worker's primary role is to generate data and automate their own job away. But, for this very reason, microwork can also point to a world where the wage disappears, where work is less central to our lives, and where we have more choice over when we work and what we work on. To paraphrase the words of the historian E. P. Thompson, this world will not rise like the sun at an appointed time; it will have to be made.[16] In the growing number of struggles across the globe, its glimmer grows ever stronger. In the fever dreams of a system entering permanent night are the blinking lights of a new dawn.

Acknowledgements

My first debt of gratitude is owed to my editor at Verso, John Merrick, whose patience, interest and support made the book possible. I am grateful to all those who, in addition to John, worked on this book, particularly Leo Hollis and Duncan Ranslem. Thank you to James Muldoon, Mitch Pass and Trahearne Falvey, whose thoughtful readings of early drafts helped shape it into something better, or else simply encouraged me to carry on. Gratitude is also owed to Will Stronge, without whose initial encouragement and generosity this book might not have been written. Thanks to Maisie Ridgway, Kat Sinclair and Elly Clarke and the rest of the Digital Technology Reading Group; our discussions are very much present in these pages. Special thanks are owed to Isabella Cipirska, Paul Williams and Sam Briggs, who regularly heard my gripes and worries about the writing process and supported me in my research every step of the way. Your continued enthusiasm proved contagious. My work was also made possible by the encouragement, interest and reading suggestions of many, including Richard Godden, Annie McClanahan, Nick Srnicek, Julian Siravo, Doug Haynes, Natalia Cecire and Aaron Benanav. Thank you also to Katie Hanlon and Matthew McConkey for Brighton book club, and Mike Jones for London book club. Thank you to the rest of my Brighton friends – James Kelly, Leah Caprio, Rhiannon Scott, Richie Maslin, Joe Trueman, Simon Jeavons, Grace Marshall, Louie Londt and Marius

Holtan, who make the bad times bearable and the good times better. Thank you to those who have known me longest – Tomos Hughes, Ruth Wallbank, Alex Shenton, Ciara Shenton, Rich Dooley, Amy Chevin, Pete Bray, Rhian Hughes, Mabli Godden, Scott Ralph and Cath Ralph. A final thank you to Rich Jones, Zillah Holford, Tony Jones and Penny Vincent, who have remained supportive every step of the way.

This book is dedicated to my partner Isa, who reminds me that a better world is possible.

Notes

Introduction

1 Naomi Klein, 'How Big Tech Plans to Profit from the Pandemic', *The Guardian*, 13 May 2020.

2 Moritz Altenreid, 'The Platform as Factory: Crowdwork and the Hidden Labour behind Artificial Intelligence', *Capital and Class* 44(2), 2020.

3 Mike Davis, *Planet of Slums*, Verso, 2006, p. 174.

4 Siddharth Mall, 'Top Playment Players Are Spending More Time on the App Than on Social Media', Linked In, 27 February 2017.

5 See Sarah O'Connor, 'The Human Cloud: A New World of Work', *Financial Times*, 8 October 2015; Jeremias Prassl, *Humans-as-a-Service: The Promise and Perils of Work in the Gig Economy*, Oxford University Press, 2018; Valerio De Stefano, 'The Rise of the "Just-in-Time Workforce": On-Demand Work, Crowdwork and Labour Protection in the "Gig-Economy"', International Labour Organization, 2016. See also 'Digital Labour Platforms and the Future of Work: Towards Decent Work in the Online World', International Labour Organization, 2018.

6 'What Is Mechanical Turk?', Pew Research, 11 July 2016.

7 Vili Lehdonvirta, 'From Millions of Tasks to Thousands of Jobs: Bringing Digital Work to Developing Countries', World Bank, 31 January 2012. See also 'The Global Opportunity in Online Outsourcing', World Bank, June 2015.

8 Mary L. Gray and Siddharth Suri, *Ghost Work: How to Stop Silicon Valley from Building a New Global Underclass*, Houghton Mifflin Harcourt USA, 2019, p. xxiv.

9 'Digital Labour Platforms', p. 88.

10 'Platform Work in the UK 2016–2019', TUC and University of Hertfordshire, 2019.

11 Ibid.

12 'Digital Labour Platforms', p. xvii.

13 Zhubajie offers a range of paid online work ranging from macroprojects to microtasks. There are no figures for how much of the work offered is actually microwork. See 'The Global Opportunity'.

14 Kotaro Hara, Abi Adams, Kristy Milland, Saiph Savage, Chris Callison-Burch, and Jeffrey P. Bigham, 'A Data-Driven Analysis of Workers' Earnings on Amazon Mechanical Turk', *Proceedings of the 2018 CHI Conference: Human Factors in Computing Systems*, April 2018, pp. 1–14.

15 For Marx's understanding of technology replacing workers and the growth of the relative surplus populations, see Karl Marx, *Capital Volume 1*, Penguin Classics, 1990, pp. 794–800. See also Karl Marx, *Grundrisse*, Penguin Classics, 1993, pp. 694–5, 704–6.

16 For the most comprehensive account of 'platform capitalism', see Nick Srnicek, *Platform Capitalism*, Polity, 2016.

17 Srnicek, *Platform Capitalism*, pp. 43–4.

18 Gray and Suri, *Ghost Work*, p. 38.

19 Lilly Irani, 'Justice for Data Janitors', Public Books, 15 January 2015.

20 For an account of 'fully automated luxury communism', see Aaron Bastani, *Fully Automated Luxury Communism*, Verso, 2019.

1 The Surplus of Silicon Valley

1 Stephanie Hegarty, 'How Silicon Valley Outsources Work to African Refugees', BBC, 18 June 2011.

2 Ruchi Gupta, 'How Much Does Jeff Bezos Make a Second', *Market Realist*, 13 August 2020.

3 Miranda Hall, 'The Ghost of the Mechanical Turk', *Jacobin*, 16 December 2017.

4 The opacity of the outsourcing process makes it difficult to say with any certainty which platform these workers are using, but for an example of a drone data training platform

that sources workers from across the Middle East, see scale. com/drones.

5 Vili Lehdonvirta, 'From Millions of Tasks to Thousands of Jobs: Bringing Digital Work to Developing Countries', World Bank, 31 January 2012.

6 Nicola Croce, 'The New Assembly Lines: Why AI Needs Low Skill Workers Too', We Forum, 12 August 2019.

7 Joel Ross, Lilly Irani, M. Six Silberman, Andrew Zaldivar, and Bill Tomlinson, 'Who Are the Crowdworkers? Shifting Demographics in Amazon Mechanical Turk', *CHI EA '10: CHI '10 Extended Abstracts on Human Factors in Computing Systems*, April 2010, pp. 2863–72.

8 For the original use of 'bare life', see Giorgio Agamben, *Homo Sacer: Sovereign Power and Bare Life*, Stanford University Press, 1998.

9 For a thorough examination of the prison-industrial complex, see Ruth Wilson Gilmore, *Golden Gulag: Prisons, Surplus, Crisis and Opposition in Globalizing California*, University of California Press, 2007, pp. 113–15.

10 Leilah Janah, 'The Virtual Assembly Line', Huffpost, 26 May 2010.

11 Dave Lee, 'Why Big Tech Pays Poor Kenyans to Teach Self-Driving Cars', BBC, 3 November 2018.

12 Ed Garstein, 'Sharp Growth in Autonomous Car Market Predicted but May Be Stalled by Rise in Consumer Fear', *Forbes*, 13 August 2018.

13 Angela Chen, 'Desperate Venezuelans Are Making Money by Training AI for Self-Driving Cars', *MIT Technology Review*, 22 August 2019.

14 Ibid.

15 John Burnett, *Idle Hands: The Experience of Unemployment 1790–1990*, Routledge, 1994, p. 170.

16 Leilah Janah, 'How Online Work Can Save America', *Tech Crunch*, 21 February 2011.

17 Frank Snowden, *Naples in the Time of Cholera*, Cambridge University Press, 1995, pp. 35–6.

18 Alex Nguyen, 'Six Weird Crowdsourcing Tasks from Amazon Mechanical Turk', Lionsbridge, 21 January 2019.

19 'World Bank Promotes Microwork Opportunities for Jobless Palestinians', World Bank, 26 March 2013.

20 Angela Chen, 'Inmates in Finland Are Training AI as Part of Prison Labour', The Verge, 28 March 2019.

21 Ibid.

22 Deborah Carey, 'Microwork: A New Approach for Labour Disparities', World Mind, 9 December 2016.

23 Lilly Irani, 'Justice for Data Janitors', Public Books, 15 January 2015.

24 Karl Marx, Capital Volume 1, Penguin Classics, 1990, p. 794.

25 For a version of this argument, see Aaron Bastani, Fully Automated Luxury Communism, Verso, 2019.

26 Aaron Benanav, 'Automation and the Future of Work – I', New Left Review, September/October 2019, p. 15.

27 Robert Brenner, The Boom and the Bubble, Verso, 2002, pp. 12–20.

28 Ibid. See also Larry Summers, Secular Stagnation, Penguin, 2019.

29 Brenner, The Boom and the Bubble, pp. 18–20

30 Benanav, 'Automation and the Future of Work – I', p. 17

31 All data on manufacturing, value added as a percentage of GDP, derived from World Bank. Last updated 2019.

32 Marx, Capital Volume 1, pp. 794–5.

33 'Misery and Debt', Endnotes, April 2010.

34 For an example of this argument, see Carl Benedikt Frey, The Technology Trap: Capital, Labor, and Power in the Age of Automation, Princeton University Press, 2019, pp. 246–8.

35 'Misery and Debt'.

36 For a description of the 'absolute general law of capitalist accumulation', see Marx, Capital Volume 1, pp. 798–802.

37 For versions of this argument, see Nick Srnicek and Alex Williams, Inventing the Future: Postcapitalism and a World without Work, Verso, 2015. See also Bastani, Fully Automated Luxury Communism.

38 For a consideration of the Solow Productivity Paradox, see Jack Triplett, 'The Solow Productivity Paradox: What Do Computers Do to Productivity?', The Canadian Journal of Economics 32(2), 1999.

39 See Brenner, The Boom and the Bubble.

40 Aaron Benanav, 'Automation and the Future of Work – 2', New Left Review, November/December 2019, p. 121.

41 Robert Rowthorn and Ramana Ramaswamy, 'Deindustriali-zation: Its Causes and Implications', IMF, September 1997.

42 Srnicek and Williams, *Inventing the Future*, p. 91.

43 Data from OECD Unemployment Rate Indicators. Last updated 2020.

44 Aaron Benanav, 'Precarity Rising', *Viewpoint Magazine*, 15 June 2015.

45 Olivier Blanchard et al., 'European Unemployment: The Evo-lution of Facts and Ideas', *Economic Policy* 21(45), 2006.

46 Jason E. Smith, *Smart Machines and Service Work: Automa-tion in an Age of Stagnation*, Reaktion Books, 2020, p. 76.

47 Anna Syed, 'Changes in the Economy since the 1970s', UK Office for National Statistics, 2 September 2019.

48 William Baumol, 'Macroeconomics of Unbalanced Growth: Anatomy of the Urban Crisis', *American Economic Review* 67(3), 1967, pp. 415–26.

49 Smith, *Smart Machines and Service Work*, p. 122.

50 See Guy Standing, *The Precariat: The New Dangerous Class*, Bloomsbury, 2016. Also see Mariele Pfannebecker and James Smith, *Work Want Work*, Zed, 2020, p. 60. For the original use of 'subemployment', see Thomas Vietor-isz, Robert Meir, and Jean-Ellen Giblin, 'Subemployment: Exclusion and Inadequacy Indexes', *Monthly Labor Review* 98, May 1975, pp. 3–12.

51 Walter Hanesch, 'In-Work Poverty in Germany', European Social Policy Network, 2019.

52 Ivor Southwood, *Non-Stop Intertia*, Zero Books, 2011.

53 Jess Staufenberg and Jon Stone, 'Revealed: The High Street Firms That Used Benefit Claimants as Free Labour', *Inde-pendent*, 31 July 2016.

54 Leigh Claire La Berge, 'Decommodified Labor: Conceptu-alizing Work after the Wage', *Lateral* 7(1), Special issue: Marxism and Cultural Studies, Spring 2018.

55 Ibid.

56 For the original use of the term, see Gosta Esping Andersen, *The Three Worlds of Welfare Capitalism*, Polity, 1990.

57 La Berge, 'Decommodified Labor'.

58 Gilmore, *Golden Gulag*.

59 Phil Neel, *Hinterland: America's New Landscape of Class and Conflict*, Reaktion Books, 2018, pp. 69–70.

60 'More Than 60 Per cent of the World's Employed Population Are in the Informal Economy', International Labour Organization, 30 April 2018.

61 Mike Davis, *Planet of Slums*, Verso, 2007, p. 175.

62 For a fuller definition of 'wage hunters and gatherers', see Jan Breman, *Wage Hunters and Gatherers: Search for Work in the Rural and Urban Economy of South Gujarat*, Oxford University Press India, 1994.

63 Davis, *Planet of Slums*, p. 178.

64 'Walmart's Global Track Record and the Implications for FDI in Multi-Brand Retail in India', UNI Global Union, March 2012. For a recent example of larger companies' use of kiranas, see Rahul Sachitanand, 'Battleground Kirana: The Anatomy of India's Raging Retail War', *The Economic Times*, 9 June 2019.

65 For an example of the World Bank's use of 'microentrepreneur', see 'Shortening Microentrepreneur Supply Chain through Mobile Technology', World Bank, 10 November 2017. For an example of the World Bank using 'microentrepreneur' in the context of microwork, see Solutions for Youth Employment, 'Digital Jobs for Youth: Young Women in the Digital Economy', World Bank, September 2018.

2 Artificial or Human Intelligence?

1 Edgar Allan Poe, 'Maelzel's Chess Player', *Southern Literary Messenger*, April 1836. Available online at The Edgar Allan Poe Society of Baltimore.

2 Shanhong Liu, 'Revenues from the Artificial Intelligence (AI) Software Market Worldwide from 2018 to 2025', Statista, 7 December 2020.

3 Nick Srnicek, *Platform Capitalism*, Polity, 2016, pp. 39–40.

4 Carl Benedikt Frey, *The Technology Trap: Capital, Labor, and Power in the Age of Automation*, Princeton University Press, 2019, pp. 301–3.

5 Ljubica Nedelkoska and Glenda Quintini, 'Automation, Skills Use and Training', *OECD Social, Employment and Migration Working Papers*, no. 202, 2018.

6 Jason Smith, 'Nowhere to Go: Automation Then and Now Part 2', *Brooklyn Rail*, April 2017.

7 Nick Dyer Witheford, Atle Mikkola Kjøsen, and James Steinhoff, *Inhuman Power: Artificial Intelligence and the Future of Capitalism*, Pluto, 2019, p. 83.

8 Gwyn Topham, 'It's Going to Be a Revolution: Driverless Cars in a London Trial', *The Guardian*, 3 October 2019.

9 Nanette Byrnes, 'As Goldman Embraces Automation, Even the Masters of the Universe Are Threatened', *Technoogy Review*, 7 February 2017.

10 Simon Chandler, 'Coronavirus Is Forcing Companies to Speed Up Automation, for Better and for Worse', *Forbes*, 12 May 2020.

11 Sasha Lekach, 'It Took a Coronavirus Outbreak for Self-Driving Cars to Become More Appealing', *Mashable*, 2 April 2020.

12 Astra Taylor, 'The Automation Charade' *Logic* 5, 1 August 2018.

13 Ibid.

14 Aaron Benanav, *Automation and the Future of Work*, Verso, 2020.

15 Aaron Benanav, *Automation and the Future of Work*, Verso, 2020, p. 6, quoting Kurt Vonnegut, *Player Piano*, Dial Press, 2006, p.73.

16 Mark Graham and Jamie Woodcock, *The Gig Economy: A Critical Introduction*, Polity, 2019, p. 54.

17 See 'Creating Chatbots and Virtual Assistants that Really Work', Appen, 10 September 2019.

18 James Vincent, 'Twitter Taught Microsoft's AI Chatbot to Be a Racist Asshole in Less Than a Day', The Verge, 24 March 2016.

19 'Twitter Improves Search with Real-Time Human Computation', Amazon Mechanical Turk, 9 January 2013.

20 Phil Jones, 'Migrant Labour without Migration', Verso Books blog, 10 June 2020.

21 Lilly Irani and M. Six Silberman, 'Turkopticon: Interrupting Worker Invisibility in Amazon Mechanical Turk', *Proceedings of CHI 2013: Changing Perspectives*, 2013, p. 612.

22 Phil Jones, 'Rethinking Microwork: The Invisible Labour of the Platform Economy', Autonomy, 2020.

23 Ibid.

24 Paola Tubaro, Antonio A. Casilli, and Marion Coville, 'The Trainer, the Verifier, the Imitator: Three Ways in Which Human Platform Workers Support Artificial Intelligence', *Big Data and Society*, January 2020.

25 'Lionsbridge Augments Artificial Intelligence Offering through Acquisition of Gengo and Gengo.Ai', Lionsbridge, 20 November 2019.

26 For an in-depth study of content moderation on platforms like Google and Facebook, see Sarah Roberts, *Behind the Screen: Content Moderation in the Shadows of Social Media*, Yale University Press, 2019.

27 'Twitter Improves Search'.

3 Human-as-a-Service

1 Vili Lehdonvirta, 'From Millions of Tasks to Thousands of Jobs: Bringing Digital Work to Developing Countries', World Bank, 31 January 2012.

2 See Leilah Janah, 'Give Work: Reversing Poverty One Job at a Time', Portfolio, 2017.

3 'Game-Changing Opportunities for Youth Employment in the Middle East and North Africa', World Bank, March 2011.

4 Franscesca Gin and Bradley Staats, 'The Microwork Solution', *The Harvard Review*, December 2012.

5 'Digital Labour Platforms and the Future of Work: Towards Decent Work in the Online World', International Labour Organization, 2018, p. 95.

6 Mary L. Gray and Siddharth Suri, *Ghost Work: How to Stop Silicon Valley from Building a New Global Underclass*, Houghton Mifflin Harcourt USA, 2019, pp. 110–13.

7 Adam Greenfield, *Radical Technologies*, Verso, 2017, p. 294.

8 Niels Van Doorn, 'From a Wage to a Wager: Dynamic Pricing in the Gig Economy', Autonomy, 2020.

9 Juliet Webster, 'Microworkers of the Gig Economy: Separate and Precarious', *New Labor Forum* 25(3), 2016, p. 58.

10 Gray and Suri, *Ghost Work*, p. 90.

11 'Digital Labour Platforms', p. 74.

12 Melinda Cooper, 'Workfare, Familyfare, Godfare: Transforming Contingency into Necessity', *South Atlantic Quarterly* 111(4), 2012, p. 646.

13 Nancy Fraser, 'Behind Marx's Hidden Abode', *New Left Review* 86, March/April 2014.

14 Sylvia Federici, 'Wages against Housework', in *Revolution at Point Zero*, PM Press, 2012, p. 16. There is a strong argument made by many social movements over the twentieth century that reducing work to only those activities that are waged ultimately fails to account for a great many laborious activities that would otherwise constitute the doer as worker. In other words, the wage might not be the best metric by which to measure which activities count as work. Most obviously, wages are not extended to the reproductive labour of care and housework.

15 Kotaro Hara, Abi Adams, Kristy Milland, Saiph Savage, Chris Callison-Burch, and Jeffrey P. Bigham, 'A Data-Driven Analysis of Workers's Earnings on Amazon Mechanical Turk', *Proceedings of the 2018 CHI Conference: Human Factors in Computing Systems*, April 2018, pp. 1–14.

16 Karl Marx, *Capital Volume 1*, Penguin Classics, 1990, pp. 697–8.

17 Alexander J. Quinn, Benjamin B. Bederson, Tom Yeh, and Jimmy Lin, 'CrowdFlow: Integrating Machine Learning with Mechanical Turk for Speed-Cost-Quality Flexibility', Human Computer Interaction Lab, 2020.

18 Veena Dubal, 'Digital Piecework', *Dissent*, Fall 2020.

19 Frank Snowden, *Naples in the Time of Cholera*, Cambridge University Press, 1995, pp. 35–6.

20 Alex J. Wood, Mark Graham, Vili Lehdonvirta, and Isis Hjorth, 'Good Gig, Bad Gig: Autonomy and Algorithmic Control in the Global Gig Economy', *Work, Employment and Society* 33(1), February 2019, p. 67.

21 Yolanda Redrup, 'Appen to Become Global Leader after $105million Leapforce Acquisition', *Financial Review*, 29 November 2017.

22 Annalee Newitz, 'The Secret Lives of Google Raters', Ars Technica, 27 April 2017.

23 M. Six Silberman and Lilly Irani, 'Operating an Employer Reputation System: Lessons from Turkopticon, 2008–2015',

Comparative Labor Law and Policy Journal 37(3), Spring 2016, p. 505.

24 For a comprehensive account of the 1934 general strike, see J. C. Irons, *Testing the New Deal: The General Textile Strike of 1934 in the American South*, University of Illinois Press, 2000.

25 Lilly Irani and M. Six Silberman, 'Turkopticon: Interrupting Worker Invisibility in Amazon Mechanical Turk', *Proceedings of CHI 2013: Changing Perspectives*, 2013.

26 Gray and Suri, *Ghost Work*, pp. 85–91.

27 Ibid.

28 E. P. Thompson, 'Time, Work-Discipline and Industrial Capitalism', *Past and Present* 38(1), 1967, p. 90.

29 'Digital Labour Platforms', p. 74.

30 Lauren Weber and Rachel Emma Silverman, 'On Demand Workers: We Are Not Robots', *Wall Street Journal*, 27 January 2015.

31 Jeff Bezos has stated he hopes for Amazon to be the 'everything store'. See Brad Stone, *The Everything Store: Jeff Bezos and the Age of Amazon*, Corgi, 2014.

32 For a list of countries to which Amazon grants the use of bank transfers, see 'Amazon Mechanical Turk Workers in 25 Countries outside of the US Can Now Transfer Their Earnings to Bank Accounts', Amazon Mechanical Turk, 1 May 2019.

33 Gray and Suri, *Ghost Work*, pp. 124–5.

34 See Jeremias Prassl, *Humans-as-a-Service: The Promise and Perils of Work in the Gig Economy*, Oxford University Press, 2018.

35 Marx, *Capital Volume 1*, p. 457.

36 Andre Gorz, *Farewell to the Working Class: An Essay on Post-Industrial Socialism*, Pluto, 1982, p. 99.

37 Raymond Williams describes culture as the material that makes up a 'way of life'; see Raymond Williams, *Marxism and Literature*, Oxford University Press, 1986, p. 19. For a lengthier discussion of the tasks undertaken by data workers on Lionsbridge, see Paola Tubaro, Antonio A. Casilli, and Marion Coville, 'The Trainer, the Verifier, the Imitator: Three Ways in Which Human Platform Workers Support Artificial Intelligence', *Big Data and Society*, January 2020, p. 6.

38 Gray and Suri, *Ghost Work*, pp. xv–xvi.

39 Gray and Suri use the site CrowdFlower in their example. I instead use Appen because CrowdFlower was acquired by Figure Eight, which was soon after acquired by Appen. See Gray and Suri, *Ghost Work*, pp. xv–xvi.

40 Perry Anderson, *The Origins of Postmodernity*, Verso, 1998, p. 85.

41 'Employment in Services (per cent of total employment)', World Bank, reprinted by International Labour Organization, 20 September 2020.

42 Lehdonvirta, 'From Millions of Tasks'.

43 Mike Davis, *Planet of Slums*, Verso, 2006, p. 181.

4 Grave Work

1 For information about Scale's automated drone services and the countries where the platform operates, see scale.com/drones.

2 James Bridle, *New Dark Age: Technology and the End of the Future*, Verso, 2019.

3 In the edition of *Capital Volume 1* used throughout this book, the passage is translated, 'They do this without being aware of it'. See Karl Marx, *Capital Volume 1*, Penguin Classics, 1990, pp. 166–7. For the translation I have used above, as well as the surrounding context, see Karl Marx, *Value: Studies by Karl Marx*, trans. Albert Dragtedt, New Park Publications, 1976, pp. 7–40.

4 Trebor Scholtz, *Uberworked and Underpaid: How Workers Are Disrupting the Digital Economy*, Polity, 2016, p. 19.

5 Lee Fang, 'Google Hired Gig Economy Workers to Improve Artificial Intelligence In Controversial Drone Targeting Project', The Intercept, 4 February 2019.

6 Ibid.

7 Makena Kelly, 'Google Hired Microworkers to Train Its Controversial Project Maven AI', The Verge, 4 February 2019.

8 Paola Tubaro, Antonio A. Casilli, and Marion Coville, 'The Trainer, the Verifier, the Imitator: Three Ways in Which Human Platform Workers Support Artificial Intelligence', *Big Data and Society*, January 2020, p. 6.

9 See Christian Sandvig, Kevin Hamilton, Karrie Karahalios, and Cedric Langbort, 'When the Algorithm Itself Is a Racist: Diagnosing Ethical Harm in the Basic Components of Software', *International Journal of Communication* 10, 2016.

10 Kevin Rector and Richard Winton, 'Despite Past Denials, LAPD Has Used Facial Recognition Software 30,000 Times in Last Decade, Records Show', *Los Angeles Times*, 21 September 2020.

11 Helen Davidson, 'Alibaba Offered Clients Facial Recognition to Identify Uighar People, Report Reveals', *The Guardian*, 17 December 2020.

12 Alex Nguyen, 'Six Weird Crowdsourcing Tasks from Amazon Mechanical Turk', Lionsbridge, 21 January 2019.

13 Karen Hao, 'The Two-Year Fight to Stop Amazon from Selling Face Recognition to the Police', MIT Technology Review, 12 June 2020.

14 Ibid.

15 Kim Lyons, 'ICE Just Signed a Contract with Facial Recognition Company Clearview AI', The Verge, 14 August 2020.

16 Paola Tubaro and Antonio Casilli, 'Micro-Work, Artificial Intelligence and the Automotive Industry', *Journal of Industrial and Business Economics* 46, 2019.

17 'Don't be evil', sometimes expressed as 'Do no evil', is the adage that once formed Google's code of employee conduct.

18 Mary L. Gray and Siddharth Suri, *Ghost Work: How to Stop Silicon Valley from Building a New Global Underclass*, Houghton Mifflin Harcourt USA, 2019, p. 16.

19 Ibid.

20 Frank Pasquale, *The Black Box Society: The Secret Algorithms That Control Information and Money*, Harvard University Press, 2016.

21 Pasquale, *The Black Box*, pp. 3–4.

22 Lily Irani, 'Difference and Dependence Among Digital Workers', *South Atlantic Quarterly*, 2015, 114 (1), pp. 225–34, p. 231.

23 Naomi Klein, 'How Big Tech Plans to Profit from the Pandemic', *The Guardian*, 13 May 2020.

24 See Amazon Mechanical Turk's 'participation agreement' at mturk.com/participation-agreement.

25 For a broader definition of 'labour broker', see Guy Standing,

The Corruption of Capitalism: Why Rentiers Thrive and Work Does Not Pay, Biteback Publishing, 2017, p. 209.

26 See Playment's privacy policy at playment.gitbook.io/legal/privacy-policy.

27 Ibid.

28 Niels Van Doorn and Adam Badger, 'Platform Capitalism's Hidden Abode: Producing Data Assets in the Gig Economy', *Antipode* 52(5), 2020, p. 1477.

29 For this argument, see Moritz Altenreid, 'The Platform as Factory: Crowdwork and the Hidden Labour behind Artificial Intelligence', *Capital and Class* 44(2), 2020.

30 Huizhong Wu, 'China Is Achieving AI Dominance by Relying on Young Blue-Collar Workers', *Vice*, 21 December 2018.

31 Ibid.

32 'China's Success at AI Has Relied on Good Data', Technology Quarterly, *The Economist*, 2 January 2020.

33 A. Aneesh, 'Global Labour: Algocratic Modes of Organisation', *Sociological Theory* 27(4), 2009.

34 On the ways cross-subsidisation is used throughout platform capitalism as a tool for data extraction, see Nick Srnicek, *Platform Capitalism*, Polity, 2016, pp. 61–2.

35 Malcolm Harris, 'The Singular Pursuit of Comrade Bezos', Medium, 15 February 2018.

36 Kim Moody, 'Amazon: Context, Structure and Vulnerability', in Jake Alimahomed and Ellen Reese, eds, *The Cost of Free Shipping: Amazon in the Global Economy*, Pluto, 2020.

37 Srnicek, *Platform Capitalism*, p. 62.

38 See Amazon Web Services, 'Global Infracture', at aws.amazon.com/about-aws/global-infrastructure.

39 Richard Seymour, *The Twittering Machine*, Verso, 2020, p. 23.

40 See Russell Brandom, 'Google, Facebook, Microsoft and Twitter Partner for Ambitious New Data Project', The Verge, 20 June 2018. See also Alex Hern, '"Partnership on AI" Formed by Google, Facebook, Amazon, IBM and Microsoft', *The Guardian*, 28 September 2016.

41 Jason E. Smith, 'Nowhere to Go: Automation, Then and Now Part 2', *Brooklyn Rail*, April 2017.

42 Nick Land, 'A Quick and Dirty Introduction to Accelerationism', *Jacobite*, 25 May 2017.

43 Nick Dyer Witheford, Atle Mikkola Kjøsen, and James Steinhoff, *Inhuman Power: Artificial Intelligence and the Future of Capitalism*, Pluto, 2019, p. 157.

44 Davey Alba, 'The Hidden Laborers Training AI to Keep Hateful Ads off Youtube Videos', *Wired*, 21 April 2017.

45 'Misery and Debt', *Endnotes*, April 2010.

5 Wageless Struggle

1 For the most influential accounts of the 'lumpenproletariat' as a section of the proletariat at risk of falling into the hands of reactionary forces, see Karl Marx and Friedrich Engels, *The Communist Manifesto*, Penguin Classics, 2002, p. 231. See also Frantz Fanon, *The Wretched of the Earth*, Penguin Classics, 2001, pp. 103, 109.

2 Guy Standing, *The Precariat: The New Dangerous Class*, Bloomsbury, 2016, p. vii.

3 Fbcontentmods, 'This Is a Message of Solidarity...', Medium, 8 June 2020.

4 Mike Davis, *Planet of Slums*, Verso, 2007, p. 199.

5 Callum Cant, *Riding for Deliveroo: Resistance in the New Economy*, Polity Press, 2019, p. 104.

6 Callum Cant, 'Deliveroo Workers Launch New Strike Wave', Notes from Below, 28 September 2019.

7 Niloufar Salehi, Lilly Irani, Michael Bernstein, Ali Alkhatib, Eva Ogbe, Kristy Milland, and Clickhappier, 'We Are Dynamo: Overcoming Stalling and Friction in Collective Action for Crowd Workers', *CHI '15: Proceedings of the 33rd Annual ACM Conference on Human Factors in Computing Systems*, 2015.

8 Lilly Irani and M. Six Silberman, 'Turkopticon: Interrupting Worker Invisibility in Amazon Mechanical Turk', *Proceedings of CHI 2013: Changing Perspectives*, 2013, pp. 612–15.

9 Salehi et al., 'We Are Dynamo'.

10 Mark Harris, 'Amazon's Mechanical Turk Workers Protest: "I Am a Human Being, Not an Algorithm"', *The Guardian*, 3 December 2014.

11 Salehi et al., 'We Are Dynamo'.

12 Miranda Katz, 'Amazon's Turker Crowd Has Had Enough', Wired, 23 August 2017.

13 Joshua Clover, Riot Strike Riot, Verso, 2016, p. 170.

14 See Clover, Riot Strike Riot. Offering a more nuanced understanding of riot and strike than usual distinctions of disorderly versus orderly, violent versus disciplined, or illegal versus legitimate, Clover carefully differentiates their respective arenas of conflict (circulation vs. production); their core activities (looting and blockading streets and highways vs. machine-breaking and impeding the workplace); and their respective objectives (fixing the price of goods vs. fixing the price of the wage).

15 Fanon, Wretched of the Earth.

16 'Two Killed as Kenyan Police Try to Quell Riot in Packed Refugee Camp,' UN News, 1 July 2011.

17 Jason Gutierrez, '"Will We Die Hungry?' A Teeming Manila Slum Chafes under Lockdown', New York Times, 17 April 2020.

18 Clover, Riot Strike Riot, p. 154. Throughout the chapter 'Surplus Rebellions', the riot repeatedly appears as the subject of history. Also see Alberto Toscano, 'Limits to Periodization,' Viewpoint Magazine, 6 September 2016.

19 See Federico Rossi, The Poor's Struggle for Political Incorporation: The Piquetero Movement in Argentina, Cambridge University Press, 2017.

20 See 'Workers Left Jobless Block Tangail-Mymensingh Highway for Food', The Daily Star, 27 April 2020. Also see 'Unemployed Workers Block Russian Highway', RadioFreeEurope RadioLiberty, 10 July 2009.

21 'Rickshaw Pullers Lift Block from Dhakar Streets', The Daily Star, 9 July 2019.

22 Marta Marello and Ann Helwege, 'Solid Waste Management and Social Inclusion of Waste Pickers: Opportunities and Challenges', Latin American Perspectives 45(1), 2018.

23 Rina Agarwala, Informal Labor, Formal Politics, and Dignified Discontent in India, University of Cambridge Press, 2013.

24 Callum Cant, 'The Frontline of the Struggle against Platform Capitalism Lies in São Paulo', Novara Media, 3 October 2020.

25 Martha Pskowski, '"They Aren't Anything without Us": Gig Workers Are Striking throughout Latin America', Vice, 11 August 2020.

26 Ibid.

27 'Uber, Taxify Drivers Strike over "Slavery-Like" Conditions', Independent Online, 13 November 2018. Also see Adiya Ray, 'Unrest in India's Gig Economy: Ola-Uber Drivers' Strike and Worker Organisation', Futures of Work, 9 December 2019.

28 See 'Protesting Uber Drivers Blockade Access to Paris Airports', The Local FR, 23 December 2016. And also see Sanjana Varghese, 'Like the Gilets Jaunes, London's Black Cab and Uber Drivers Rail against Environmental Policy', Wired, 1 April 2019.

29 E. P. Thompson. The Making of the English Working Class, Penguin, 1991, p. 604.

30 For a more comprehensive account of Luddism, see Thompson, The Making of the English Working Class, pp. 605–45.

31 Paul Mason, Postcapitalism: A Guide to Our Future, Penguin, 2016, pp. 114–15.

32 Marx and Engels, The Communist Manifesto, p. 231.

33 'How the National Unemployed Workers' Movement emerged' can be found in: John Burnett, Idle Hands: The Experience of Unemployment 1790–1990, Routledge, 1994, pp. 255–6.

34 Marcus Barnett, 'Unemployed Workers Can Fight Back', Jacobin, 18 July 2020.

35 Wal Hannington, 'Fascist Danger and the Unemployed', National Unemployed Workers' Movement, 1939.

36 Ralph Hayburn, 'The National Unemployed Workers' Movement, 1921–36', International Review of Social History 28(3), 1983, p. 286. See also Raphael Samuel, The Lost World of British Communism, Verso, 2006.

37 Cibele Rizek and André Dal'Bó, 'The Growth of Brazil's Homeless Workers' Movement', Global Dialogue: Magazine of the International Sociological Association 5(1), 2015.

38 For a discussion of the group's role in protesting the Brazilian World Cup and the impeachment of the former Brazilian president Dilma Rousseff, see Victor Albert and Maria

Davidenko, 'Justification Work: The Homeless Workers' Movement and the Pragmatic Sociology of Dissent in Brazil's Crisis', *European Journal of Cultural and Political Sociology* 5(1–2), 2018.

39 Paul Apostolidis, *The Fight for Time*, Oxford University Press, 2018, p. 188.

40 See Rajat Kathuria, Mansi Kedia, Gangesh Varma, Kaushambi Bagchi, and Saumitra Khullar, *The Potential and Challenges for Online Freelancing and Microwork in India*, Indian Council for Research on International Economic Relations, December 2017.

41 Fredric Jameson, *An American Utopia: Dual Power and the Universal Army*, Verso, 2016, p. 4.

42 Agarwala, *Informal Labor*, p. 33.

43 Amy Hall, 'Can't Pay, Won't Pay', *New Internationalist*, 27 May 2020.

44 Angela Giuffrida and Sam Jones, 'Italy to Unveil Lockdown Relief Package as Protests Continue', *The Guardian*, 27 October 2020.

45 Jon Stone, 'Rebecca Long Bailey Calls for National Food Service to Help People in Isolation', *The Independent*, 23 March 2020.

46 Adam D. Reich and Seth J. Prins, 'The Disciplining Effect of Mass Incarceration on Labor Organisation', *American Journal of Sociology* 125(5), March 2020.

47 Joshua Clover, '66 Days', Verso Books blog, 2 June 2020.

48 Sophie Lewis, *Full Surrogacy Now: Feminism against Family*, Verso, 2019, p. 76.

49 Aaron Benanav, *Automation and the Future of Work*, Verso, 2020, p. 99.

50 Nick Srnicek and Alex Williams, *Inventing the Future: Postcapitalism and a World without Work*, Verso, 2015.

51 For a comprehensive vision of what a green new deal would look like see Kate Aronoff, Alyssa Battistoni, Daniel Aldana Cohen and Thea Riofrancos, *A Planet to Win: Why We Need a Green New Deal*, Verso, 2019.

Postscript

1 See Aaron Bastani, *Fully Automated Luxury Communism*, Verso, 2019. See also Paul Mason, *Postcapitalism: A Guide to Our Future*, Penguin, 2016.

2 Kristin Ross, *Communal Luxury*, Verso, 2015, p. 3.

3 Ross, *Communal Luxury*.

4 Ross, *Communal Luxury*, p. 22.

5 Andrea Long Chu, 'My New Vagina Won't Make Me Happy: And It Shouldn't Have To', *New York Times*, 24 November 2018.

6 Helen Hester, *Xenofeminism*, Polity, 2018, p. 30–1.

7 William Morris, 'The Hopes of Civilization', in A. L. Morton, ed., *The Political Writings of William Morris*, Wishart, 1973, p. 175.

8 David Graeber, *Bullshit Jobs*, Simon and Schuster, 2018. Graeber uses the term to describe jobs that are pointless and are understood to be so by those who do them.

9 Andre Gorz, *Farewell to the Working Class: An Essay on Post-Industrial Socialism*, Pluto, 1982, p. 102.

10 William Morris, *Useful Work versus Useless Toil*, Judd Publishing, 1919, p. 14.

11 Morris, *Useful Work*, p. 11.

12 See Ernst Bloch, *The Principle of Hope*, MIT Press, 1995.

13 Karl Marx and Frederick Engels, *The German Ideology*, Lawrence and Wishart, 1999, p. 54.

14 Gorz, *Farewell to the Working Class*, p. 103.

15 Edward Bellamy, *Looking Backward, 2000–1887*, Oxford, 2007, pp. 39–44.

16 See E. P. Thompson, *The Making of the English Working Class*, Penguin, 1991, pp. 8–9. Of the working class, Thompson writes, 'The working class did not rise like the sun at an appointed time. It was present at its own making.